Plantation
politics

Plantation politics

Forest plantations in development

Edited by
Caroline Sargent and
Stephen Bass

EARTHSCAN
Earthscan Publications Ltd, London

First published 1992 by

Earthscan Publications Ltd
120 Pentonville Road, London N1 9JN

British Library Cataloguing-in-Publication Data

A catalogue record for this book is available from the British Library

ISBN 1-85383-113-1

Typeset by Witwell Ltd, Southport
Printed and bound by Biddles Ltd, Guildford and King's Lynn

Earthscan Publications Ltd is an editorially independent subsidiary of Kogan
Page Ltd and publishes in association with the International Institute for
Environment and Development and the World Wide Fund for Nature (UK).

CONTENTS

List of boxes and tables   6
Note on the contributors   7
Acknowledgements   8
1 Introduction   9
  Caroline Sargent
2 Natural forest or plantation?   16
  Caroline Sargent
3 Building from the past: forest plantations in history   41
  Stephen Bass
4 How much wood do we need?   76
  Alf Leslie
5 What about the people?   92
  Elaine Morrison and Stephen Bass
6 Forest plantations: towards sustainable practice   121
  Peter J. Kanowski and Peter S. Savill
7 Conclusions   156
  Stephen Bass
References   170
Index   187

LIST OF BOXES AND TABLES

Boxes

2.1 Economic transitions towards forest plantations   38
2.2 Complex plantations   39
3.1 Poplars and willows: the emergence of important plantation
     trees   69
3.2 Forest plantations in Japan's development   71
3.3 Teak plantations in Burma: a story of policy inconsistency   73
4.1 'Silvibusiness': corporate involvement in plantations – ideas
     for sustainable practice   85
4.2 Corporate plantations aiming for sustainability: Aracruz Celulose   90
5.1 Participatory and Rapid Rural Appraisal (P/RRA)   116
5.2 Industrial plantations integrating local people's interests:
     the Paper Industry Corporation of the Philippines (PICOP)   117
5.3 Gender issues in plantation feasibility studies   118
6.1 Plantations of indigenous tree species in Ghana   151
6.2 Plantations in Costa Rica   152
6.3 Development assistance for plantations   153
6.4 The United Kingdom Overseas Development Administration's
     approach to plantations   154

Tables

4.1 Projections of world consumption of industrial roundwood to
     the year 2040   80
6.1 Forest and plantation areas by region (mid-1980s)   123
6.2 Productivity (annual wood increment) of various well-managed
     forest types   125

NOTE ON THE CONTRIBUTORS

Caroline Sargent is Director of the Forestry and Land Use Programme at IIED. She is a scientist (plant ecologist) now working principally on forest policy, planning and research issues.

Stephen Bass, Associate Director, Forestry and Land Use Programme, IIED is a forester and researcher in environment and development policy.

Elaine Morrison is the Forestry and Land Use Programme Assistant. Her research interests are in forestry and development.

Peter Kanowski and **Peter Savill** are both lecturers at the Oxford Forestry Institute, Oxford University. Their research and teaching activities include forest policy, forest genetics, forest ecology and silviculture.

Alf Leslie is a retired academic and forest economist with much experience in Australia and internationally; he was previously Director of the Forest Industries Division of FAO.

ACKNOWLEDGEMENTS

The *Netherlands Ministry of Foreign Affairs* sponsored the research by IIED's Forestry and Land Use Programme that has made this book possible. We are indebted to the Ministry for its continuing support to the Programme, and to *Fritz Schlingemann, Egbert Pellinck* and *Fea Boegborn* of the Ministry for their personal interest and support.

Many other people have been very helpful to the editors and authors, and their generosity is gratefully acknowledged: *Pete Steen* and *Cheryl Oakes* of the Forest History Society, Durham, North Carolina; *Philip H. Maxwell* of the Shell International Petroleum Company Ltd, UK; *Julian Evans* of the Forestry Commission, UK; *Bill Howard* of the Overseas Development Administration, UK; *Jim Ball* of FAO; and *Professor Matti Palo* of the Finnish Forest Research Institute, for preparing Box 2.1.

Christine Barton provided valuable editorial assistance in the final stages of this book.

Caroline Sargent
Stephen Bass

London, April 1992

CHAPTER I

INTRODUCTION

Caroline Sargent

The area of land in the tropics cultivated for wood production has more than doubled during the last decade. However, there has also been a declining proportion of single-purpose industrial monoculture plantations to smaller-scale plantations with diverse purposes and ownership structures; and there have been significant failures in industrial plantations.

It is not immediately apparent why this is so. Stable demand for industrial wood from the tropics has grown. Governments in many countries have offered effective tax and investment incentives for plantations. Wood production from plantations is usually more economically viable and environmentally acceptable than from natural forest. There are vast tracts of unoccupied and degraded lands in the tropics in which trees could be grown. Plantation goods and services provide substantial benefits for local people. Plantations also protect and provide alternatives to the natural resource. Or do they? What is the problem? What has gone wrong?

Failures in industrial plantations have almost always been attributed to a mismatch between site and species, and are laid at the door of the silviculturalist and plant technician. It is certainly true that success has eluded plantations in the humid tropics and that technical reasons have been significant. There is however, a considerable body of research aiming to improve site selection and to tackle the implications of the narrow genetic base which is associated with biological instability and lack of resilience in monocultures. Where there is sufficient investment and concern, technical precautions and solutions can usually be made available. However, relatively less attention has been paid to the political issues that surround the use of land for industrial plantations. The replacement of apparently low-value natural forest by plantations, the conflicting demands with agriculture, and clashes with local individual and common-property resource and land rights, incur costs which may well outweigh any potential industrial, socio-economic or environmental benefits. However, they have seldom fully been taken into account. Research at IIED has demonstrated the prevalence and significance of these broad political issues.

For example, in Papua New Guinea, government investment in *Pinus* plantations has been largely wasted where these were established on land under dispute with local landowners. Planting and growing a tree gives tenure rights over that tree, and consequently over the soil in which it is rooted. Taungya systems, in which villagers cultivate land around trees during establishment years, were introduced. The villagers, fearing they would lose their land, gave each little pine tree a sharp tug while cultivating – effectively destroying the rooting systems and killing the saplings. In some cases, where plantations were successfully established, lack of return to the villagers and concerns about land ownership have led to wilful burning of the trees.

In Vietnam, attempts to stabilize shifting agriculture by growing industrial trees have not always been successful. A *Pinus* plantation in Hoa Binh Province was established where there was no infrastructure for extraction and transport of the trees, and where there was no local market. After some years, the trees were burnt, and food crops re-established. Considerable hardship led to confrontation with the State.

In Java, a practical recognition of the need to involve local people is manifest in the gradual development of taungya practices into long-term intercropping. As taungya developed in Indonesia, it enabled farmers to intercrop during the establishment years. Wider spacing of trees permits permanent establishment of intercrops. If intercrops are nitrogen-fixing, they may contribute to the vigour of the plantation. Costs of plantation management may be transferred to the farmer in return for use of the land, and, further, the wider spacing – as well as the vested interest of the farmer – reduces the fire risk.

In writing this book we have sought to define, and to begin to answer, fundamental questions about the rationale and purpose of industrial plantations in the developing world. Is it possible for industrial monocultures to marry national economic goals with global demands for sequestering and storing carbon; and to wed the social and environmental well-being of local communities with the essential conservation of biological diversity? Under what circumstances can this be achieved, or does such outrageous polygamy lead invariably to dissolution? We have asked whether it is generally possible to broaden the scope of industrial plantations to accommodate social and environmental needs more fully, or whether local concerns always demand more localized solutions.

We have not considered that the ethical discussion of whether or not wood and wood fibre should be used to the current extent is central to the purpose of this book. There is a large section of humanity which urgently requires more wood – for housing, energy (fuelwood) and educational (paper) purposes. Moreover, use of renewable sources of energy is generally preferable to use of fossil fuels, whilst wood from plantations used for construction purposes or furniture will provide a net environmental benefit. Carbon will be fixed and stored in the timber for a lengthy period, and the relatively large use of energy to manufacture wood substitutes will be avoided. There is also a net, if smaller, benefit in the production of paper. We ask any reader who was expecting a diatribe against the use of wood and wood fibre not, in disgust, to burn this book! Rather, to buy more copies, and to ask colleagues and friends to do the same – and to store their books in wooden bookcases.

Central, however, to this book is the concern that wood should be grown in such a way that essential and important rights to, and benefits from, land and forest resources should not be abused, and that these resources should not be wasted. Production of wood is critical to the society in which we live, and will continue to be so, even were a utopia attained in which individual wants were precisely attuned to the equitable and sustainable use of the resource. Current and projected needs for wood cannot be met from natural forest regeneration alone; plantations will be needed.

It is clear that a very wide range of enterprises could be referred to as plantations: a village woodlot; an orchard; industrial plantings of cocoa, coffee and oil palm. However, in this book we are principally concerned with large-scale industrial plantations which are committed to the production of wood and wood fibre. These are the plantations which engender particular political debate.

Those issues which are most divisive and attract most heated discussion include:

- socio-economic issues: inequitable distribution of costs and benefits; insufficient opportunity and inadequate returns for labour
- land and rights issues: loss of individual and common property rights to forest resources and land; ill-defined, uncodified or absent tenure; inappropriate and unplanned use
- environmental issues: ecological vulnerability and instability; resource scarcity; biological impoverishment; soil loss and erosion; hydrological problems; inappropriate tree and site selection
- managerial issues: inadequate plantation management and design; inappropriate policy and legislation; misdirected incentives; malfeasance.

Whilst such areas of concern are by no means restricted to the developing world, many of them attract particular political comment, and are responsible for a critical degree of hardship and environmental impoverishment in less-developed tropical nations. Hence our discussion will focus most strongly on that world, drawing on the financially more secure regions only for purposes of balanced argument and information.

What is the future for plantations in tropical countries? The political complexities suggest that it could well be preferable to grow wood in temperate countries, where, in particular, there is less social inequity, there are formalized systems of land tenure and systems of land-use planning and control which are well established. Does this mean that tropical plantations can only be considered as social and environmental welfare packages? Or can tropical plantations give adequate returns on investment, whilst promoting social and environmental well-being?

Chapter 2 sets the scene by assessing the relative merits of harvesting trees from natural forest or plantation. The relative wood productivity figures are well known, but what are the social and environmental implications of turning from a diverse natural ecosystem towards a high-input perennial crop? Current myths relating to the substitutability of plantations *vis-à-vis* natural forests and their role in protecting natural forests are examined, and the conditions under which plantations become an appropriate form of land use are explored.

Primary political concerns are the conservation of natural forests' biodiversity. To what extent does the establishment of plantations contribute to the protection of natural forests? Whilst it is clear that plantation-grown wood will substitute readily for much that can be grown in natural forests, it is altogether too simplistic to assume that if plantation wood reduces demand for wood from natural forests, trees will not be felled in natural forests and the forest will not be cleared. This is because the destructive pressure on natural forests is not exerted on the trees, but on the soil upon which the trees grow. However, where natural forest has a realizable financial value as, for example, in the production of high-value forms of timber, better opportunites for preventing complete forest conversion arise.

There are therefore very strong arguments that suggest that the establishment of plantations, where their products are in direct competition with natural forest, can have a negative effect on the retention of managed natural forest. There are also very strong arguments that show that pressure can be removed from the natural forest, and that direct protection can be provided by plantation buffer zones. What is the outcome in practice?

In Chapter 3, trends in the historical development of plantations are described and discussed with a view towards establishing lessons for modern plantation establishment and use. The scope is initially broad, examining the evolution of plantations in the classical and temperate world, then moves towards the tropics and subtropics, where a relatively recent growth of large-scale industrial plantations has been concentrated. The historical perspective describes the contributions to plantation science and practice that different actors have made in different social contexts and at different times, and explores the divergence between political and macroeconomic interests and more local concerns, shedding light on how we might more appropriately move forwards.

In many minds, development is directly related to the clearing of the forest – a practice which did, indeed, characterize early economic growth. The re-establishment of trees may well be misconstrued as economic regression, even where employment in planting and maintenance provides an immediate economic return to the community. The process of establishing a plantation in the tropics is likely to prove a major event in the lives of people in local communities, and such people will have very understandable concerns. Such concerns have readily been stimulated by radical environmental opinion, which, in pursuit of political goals have overlooked the need for a more pragmatic and balanced approach. What insights can historical analysis lend to the resolution of such problems?

Science is often said to have reached maturity when it can afford to ignore its history. Plantation science has certainly not reached such a stage, and is only beginning to explore the complexities of social and environmental interaction. Further, very little absolute information is available. Thompson, Warburton and Hatley (1986) write:

> Policy issues can be approached in two ways. You can ask 'what are the facts?' and you can ask 'what would you like the facts to be?' In a situation in which there is already considerable uncertainty about the facts the sensible approach is by way of the first question. . . . But in a situation where there is wide uncertainty about the facts the sensible approach is by way of the second question.

Chapter 4, examines the uncertainty of information and the variety of analyses and forecasts that have indicated what the demand for wood is likely to be. Some excellent data exist, but there are also large gaps, and there have been very substantial variations in the way predictions have been made – leading to correspondingly substantial variations in investment. Growers are increasingly aware of the changing nature of the world market for wood. The rate of growth of wood consumption has slowed from about 3 per cent per annum in the mid-1950s, to a little over 1 per cent at present. Locally, wood is grown for which there is no market; elsewhere demands exist that cannot be met. How is it possible to ensure that supply meets demand and the price for wood reflects the costs of good management?

Market complexities introduced by command processing, where governments attempt to create or retain local forest industries via regulation, need also to be taken into account, as do potential and real impacts of tariff and trade barriers and consumer boycotts. These clearly have a very strong impact on what should be grown and where. In many cases the interactions between and within countries require monitoring and review, to determine that the sum of effects is that which was originally intended.

Except where alternative land-use pressures are light, a principal cause of plantation failure has been inadequate attention to local peoples' concerns and interests. During the past few years it has become accepted that the provision of local employment from plantations is not a sufficient social rationale for their establishment. To ensure success, the full spectrum of local needs and dependencies on the land and resources scheduled for conversion to plantation must be taken into account. Chapter 5 describes in some detail the kinds of measures that should be taken, and reviews situations in which such measures have proved successful.

It is easy to empathize with the landless, or those whose lands have been alienated, who see trees being planted by strangers or a distant government. The trees give them little, if any, return on land which might have been cultivated for direct benefit. How different from the satisfaction of the man who owns his land and can afford to invest for the future security of his family.

Empathy alone, however, is inadequate. A solid understanding of the local situation, and a willingness to respect local rights, are essential for a satisfactory resolution. We discuss the interaction between tenure and other rights, the current and potential economic processes, and the size, structure and likely demographic trends in the population. Should certain areas of alienated land or state-owned land be reserved for plantation purposes? The arguments are essentially those that lead demands for agrarian reform. It is readily accepted that plantations should be established in areas where there is no preferred economic opportunity. It has been less readily recognized that plantations should be introduced only where they are socially acceptable, indeed socially desirable. Such acceptability will vary enormously with the culture and traditions of the people concerned.

By Chapter 6 we have reached a point where it is necessary to question where the technical state of plantation art stands in relation to what is required of plantations in sustainable development. Do we now know enough from biological, social and economic points of view to integrate our knowledge to successfully plan industrial plantations for the tropics? Are industrial plantations compatible with social and environmental needs and demands, or do alternative strategies exist? Where should research and development go?

Finally, in Chapter 7, we draw together the conclusions from all our contributors to provide what is, if not exactly a set of guidelines, at least a coherent series of points which should be addressed by the serious planner, decision maker and industrialist – and, indeed, by those whose job it is to draw attention to social injustice and environmental degradation. These conclusions draw from both the main text of the chapters and the boxes which accompany them. The material in the boxes has been prepared by the editors to accompany the text, offering a form of parallel narrative to that in illustrations and brief case studies.

In our research, we have attempted to introduce fact, and to reject unsubstantiated conjecture. However, there has been little factual, non-technical information available, especially in a form which is accessible to the concerned public and involved professionals and administrators. This book has therefore tried to distinguish what is known and what can be predicted with a reasonable degree of confidence, from what, whether through lack of information or for political purpose, has become conjecture, or even propaganda. What many of us thought we knew about plantations 'just (as Al Jolson frequently remarked) ain't so'!

CHAPTER 2

NATURAL FOREST OR PLANTATION?

Caroline Sargent

The scope of the issue

Central to all forest policies is the decision of whether wood should be grown in plantation or under natural forest management. Industrial plantations can yield of the order of 5–50 cubic metres per hectare per year, whilst **sustainable** production from natural forest may be as little as half a cubic metre (Poore 1989). However, there are social, environmental and economic problems associated with growing trees for industrial purposes. These are particularly apparent in the tropics where demands for alternative land use may be high, where capitalization of resources has outweighed investment, where individual and community rights may not be recognized, and where equitable systems for dealing with these issues are not codified or institutionalized to the extent that has occurred in more financially secure parts of the world.

Nevertheless, with increasing loss of natural sources of timber, areas of plantation have expanded rapidly since 1970. In 1940 plantations were relatively uncommon (Campbell 1991). Allan and Lanly (1991) report that the global area of plantations has increased from 81 million hectares in 1965 to an estimated 130 million hectares in 1990. FAO data indicate that in 1980 tropical plantations occupied 11.7 million hectares. By 1990 Evans considered the total area of tropical plantations had become about 35 million hectares: 'The figure is not precise but includes the imaginative social forestry programmes of India and tropical and sub-tropical China and embraces all planting for industrial, social and environmental protection purposes' (Evans 1990).

Even taking a conservative estimate of 25 million hectares of tropical plantation in 1990, this indicates at least a **doubling in area during the last decade**.

During the same period, the area of natural tropical forest was reduced from approximately 1937 million hectares to less that 1800 million hectares; a loss of over 100 million hectares (including moist and dry forest, fallows and closed and open canopy). Although the proportion of plantation to natural forest in the tropics remains small, this rose during the decade from about 0.6 per cent to 1.7 per cent. The estimated percentage proportion of plantation to natural forest world-wide is given as 3.7 per cent, indicating the relatively greater proportion of plantations in temperate and boreal areas. In Japan, 45 per cent of forests are plantations. In Germany it is believed that as little as 3 per cent of present forest cover has come from natural regeneration; here natural regeneration – the processes of chance, circumstance and competition which lead to the development or regrowth of natural forest – has been called a neolithic approach to arboriculture.

Scarcity, and predicted scarcity, of timber and pulp have led to increased investment in plantations, and this has generally been widely welcomed. However, in some quarters, there is an assumption that, irrespective of natural forest or plantation, tree cover is environmentally, socially and economically beneficial. Amongst British colonial foresters, according to one report 'any form of wooding is preferred to a grass or shrub cover, and any factor inhibiting the growth of wooded species is condemned' (Langlands 1967).

It has further been assumed that plantations provide a direct substitute for natural forests, and moreover that the establishment of plantations serves to remove pressure from natural forests and hence to protect the resource.

To what extent are these assumptions correct? The difficulties with establishing industrial monocultures in the tropics may be such that it is critical to find alternatives.

This chapter is given to a consideration of the extent to which industrial plantations:

• are socially, environmentally and economically beneficial;
• substitute directly for natural forests;
• provide protection, through economic substitution, for natural forests.

Whether there is, indeed, a choice to be made between natural forest and plantation is questioned. Are the roles so distinct that comparison is not appropriate and that relative merits should be considered independently in relation to the tropical landscape?

Definitions

The distinction between plantation and natural forest is not as clear cut as it may at first seem. There is a complex gradient between the diverse natural forest which dominates the landscape through biological processes of mutualism, competition and selection, and the monotone plantation, where control of these processes is exercised by people.

Manufactured chemicals supplement or replace nutrient cycling between tree and soil fauna; pollination and seed dispersal become irrelevant; and in a timber plantation merely the trunk is the objective. In the natural forest the trunk is the 'peacock's tail' (Harper 1977), giving the tree competitive advantage over its neighbours to raise its crown into the canopy and the sunlight.

Silvicultural activities in natural forests move the forest towards a simpler state, in which one or a few preferred timber trees predominate. This is less natural but more profitable. The widely-used terms 'classical' and 'modern' silviculture reflect this idea. Lamprecht (1990) suggests that the most important distinctions are in that:

> **Classical silviculture** seeks to achieve its objectives by the best possible sustained utilization, under controlled conditions, of the natural productive potential of a site, i.e. by objective oriented management of the ecosystem

whilst:

> **Modern silviculture** makes use mainly of artificial forests, in a way that is as independent as possible of the natural site, and in an artificial environment that can only be maintained artificially.

Thus modern, or plantation silviculture, becomes primarily a cropping activity:

> The management is agricultural. The ground is prepared and ploughed several times, one plants, prunes, thins rigorously and harvests. Then the same cycle is begun again. The soil is kept fertile artificially by using fertilisers. Insect and fungus diseases are controlled artificially by spraying as in agriculture.
>
> (Wicht 1968, quoted in Lamprecht 1990)

As with all uniform, high-input, agricultural crops, there will be a uniform response to changing circumstances. Plantations are intentionally unstable (Palmer quoted in Sargent and Bass 1992). A field of wheat may be attacked by rust, or it may lodge under high winds. At worst this will result in a single year's loss of production. A plantation on a rotation of twenty or thirty years may, however, be attacked by borer or suffer from unpredicted environmental fluctuation or change, damaging the timber;

and the investment consequences of this will be far more severe. For example, in East Africa, the cypress aphid *Cinara cupressi* has been devastating the cypress *Cupressus lusitanica*, which has been widely planted for many years.

Internal rates of return in plantation forestry are hard to predict, and indeed it is often questioned whether current economic analysis tools are adequate for long-term forestry (e.g. Mengin-Lecreux and Durand 1987). What is really being questioned is whether it is possible to predict not only changes in demand, but also environmental variations, including atmospheric pollution (cf. the significant damage to plantations in central Europe) which have less than predictable consequences.

The potential instability of plantations caused by genetic uniformity is widely recognized – but there is a further dimension to instability based on political and social acceptability. The long-term nature of plantations leads to an immensely increased vulnerability over shorter-term agricultural rotations, and hence to a very different set of problems in determining where plantations are likely to provide an appropriate form of land use.

Plantations may move towards a 'forest state' as Dawkins (1988) suggested when he defined successful tropical silviculture to be:

> when a fine stand of timber trees has been brought to maturity and is producing natural regeneration on a site where it has matured before.

Although plantations can be considered to arise from any deliberate tree-planting activity, for the purpose of this chapter, the meaning is restricted to perennial woody crops which may, under certain conditions (often linked with neglect or less intensive management!), provide some of the environmental benefits of natural forests. Further, although it is recognized that trees may be planted under a wide range of circumstances – as part of the agricultural landscape, for aesthetic pleasure or within the context of classical silviculture – and with a wide range of intended products – fuel, food, protection – the principal concern here is with industrial wood monocultures in the tropics.

Politics and ownership

Inevitably, choice in a pluralistic society is a matter of politics. Whether to manage natural forest or to grow trees *de novo* is seldom based on a rational integration of biological, social and economic knowledge – who yet does that in a convincing way? – but is buried deep in the politics of conflict resolution. The principal conflict is over who controls the land.

Land use and control

In Thailand today there is a good, but by no means unique, example of this. Wholly opposing views are held in relation to the Government's policy toward forest cover. The current (sixth) National Social and Economic Development Plan calls for a forest cover of 40 per cent. In 1989, the area of land under natural, closed canopy forest was less that 28 per cent, and legislation was introduced which aimed to halt deforestation by banning logging. In tandem, an ambitious programme of plantations (reforestation) was proposed. For the thirty-year period between 1991 and 2020, it was decided that, to achieve the 40 per cent target, 38.5 million rai (6.16 million hectares) of commercial and community forests should be established (Sargent 1990).

But why was there opposition to this? The reforestation programme was not publicized as a question of choice between plantation or natural forest, but was an attempt to halt forest loss and to improve the environment. The farmers, encouraged by the non-governmental community, were not convinced, however. Plantations are not, as the Government policy suggests, equivalent to natural forest. The policy to ban logging has not prevented deforestation. The principal cause of deforestation was, and remains, clearing of land for agricultural purposes. Many of the eight million people in Thailand who are officially considered landless are finding a meagre livelihood by clearing forest and establishing usufructuary rights to farm. With the logging ban, there are no longer loggers to defend the forests and prevent encroachment on forest land which was held under concession – and thus the natural forest continues to diminish.

The Government's remedial strategy – to establish large tracts of man-made forest – runs into the same set of land scarcity problems. Usufructuary agricultural rights are in existence over most suitable non-forested land (even within the formal Government Forest Estate), and commercial investors find difficulty in identifying land without conflicting prior claims. Farmers will not lightly cede rights to land and livelihood, and they have cited the supposed environmental disbenefits of *Eucalyptus* to crusade against the policy. The battle is not about *Eucalyptus*, however. It is about power.

Plantations are promoted as profitable and environmentally beneficial for farmers. Consider, however, the initial outlay, the lag in financial return, the uncertainty of land tenure, and the unpredictability of the future market. These leave tree-growing as a minor prospect for most farmers. Where are the trees to be planted? How and by whom? How are the natural forests to be protected?

Global demands

In this example from Thailand, the difficulties in integrating social and environmental issues, whilst deciding upon appropriate land use, are clearly apparent. The immensely ambitious plantation programme is not a balanced response to social need, nor yet to environmental or economic reality. 'Greening the environment', the phrase used in the UNCED Agenda 21 to describe the process and intention of establishing vast tracts of plantations, is politically plausible. But how sensible is it? Let us look at the global implications.

The Intergovernmental Panel on Climate Change (IPCC) predicts that global temperatures will rise by 1°C by 2025 and by 3°C before the end of the next century if no actions are taken to limit emissions of greenhouse gases (carbon dioxide, methane, CFCs and nitrous oxide) or to increase sequestration of carbon dioxide. Carbon dioxide is taken out of the atmosphere during photosynthesis, the process driven by the sun's energy in which green plants form sugars. Carbon dioxide is released during plant decomposition (including burning). Currently an excess of 3 billion tons of carbon is being emitted annually.

The IPCC estimate indicates that, before the end of the next century, the temperature will be higher than it has been for 100,000 years. Estimates of the ability of boreal forest to adapt and continue to flourish under such rapid change indicate that, unless the rate can be held to about 0.1°C per decade, there will be very substantial loss of natural forest. Less work has been done on the resilience of tropical forest, and there is little certainty about the rates at which species and biological systems will be able to evolve or respond to these very rapid rates of change. However, the considerable diversity of tropical forests indicates that, in parts, these may be more adaptable and stable than temperate or boreal ecosystems.

One strategy that has been suggested to limit temperature increase is to plant sufficient forest to mop up excess carbon dioxide. At the Ministerial Conference on Atmospheric Pollution and Climate Change held in Noordwijk in 1989, a target of global **net** increase in forest cover of 12 million hectares per annum was set in order to achieve this. The total additional area of rapidly-growing plantations which it was estimated would be needed is 400–500 million hectares, which might be established at a cost of US$ 400 per hectare. At 12 million hectares per annum this would take about forty years to achieve. However, such an equation assumes that emission levels will remain constant, and neglects compensation for the lag in emissions accumulated between now and then.

Furthermore, because deforestation continues, at rates widely estimated to lie between 14 and 20 million hectares per annum, the total area to be planted each year would have to be closer to 30 million hectares, at an annual cost of US$ 12,000 million.

The strategy also assumes that the carbon will be fixed on a relatively permanent basis. The carbon balance of a mature forest is more or less stable. What is sequestered will be compensated by what is released during natural processes of decomposition. Net long-term uptake in a mature natural forest will occur only if biomass is harvested, enabling more growth, and only if the products are prevented from decaying. Thus a well-managed natural forest from which products are used for furniture or permanent construction purposes is an extremely effective system for mopping up and storing carbon. Industrial plantations, on the other hand, whilst they sequester large quantities of carbon during rapid growth phases, are more frequently used to produce pulp for short-term purposes such as paper and packaging, and unless specific storage end-purposes are defined, may not make a significant contribution.

Changes in thinking

Such intergovernmental strategies and the finance they command empower a top-down approach to plantation establishment – but how effective can this be? There has recently been radical revision and rethinking of the role of forestry. The concept that forestry is primarily concerned with providing **national services**, in terms of protection of soil and water and industrial growth through timber production and export, began seriously to be questioned at the 8th World Forestry Congress in Jakarta (1978). Since then, a far greater emphasis has been given to **local services** and focus has been placed on the needs and rights of people whose livelihoods depend on trees and forests. Further, there has been a gathering recognition within the forestry community that people plant trees when they perceive a social or economic benefit, and that, although a need to supply technical information and financial investment may remain, a far greater focus on helping people protect and use existing forest is essential (van Ginneken 1991).

This is incompatible in most respects with the thinking that devised the Noordwijk target, and it becomes necessary to question the concept that what is good for the global community is good for the village community. In principal, planting trees is of immense benefit for all. In reality, tree planting may not be an appropriate strategy for an individual developing world farmer, and planting on the scale recommended at the Noordwijk Convention will certainly have drastic political consequences, quite apart from the effects of over-production of wood, and hence of removing economic value from natural forest production.

To return to our example in Thailand, plantations do not compete economically with agriculture. Further, there is a curious discrepancy in Government Policy that indicates 'reforestation' on the one hand to be a direct substitute for natural forest, and on the other, natural forest to be too environmentally important to convert to plantation. Moreover, there is confusion and incompatibility in the political marriage between small farmers and environmentalists. The ills of *Eucalyptus* may be used as a common banner in defending rights over cleared agricultural land, and the Government may have been encouraged to ban logging, thereby leaving the forest open to encroachment, but as yet there are only very local movements towards the appropriate use and protection of natural forest. There is no clear demonstration that rights wrested from Government are being put to better environmental use, although the immediate social benefits may be substantial.

This is not such an enigma in Sweden where natural forest has largely been lost and where:

> over the centuries . . . we have captured the entire forest landscape in active planned utilization in which different actions and age classes move around in century-long cultivation cycles.
>
> (Remrod 1991)

Perhaps so. In Sweden there are few alternative demands on the land. Structures of tenure are codified and power is equitably shared. From the biological point of view, Swedish forest ecosystems are relatively simple, being dominated by only one or a few tree species. They are therefore more readily mimicked by plantation, and cycles of clear felling and silviculture are not far removed from natural forest processes. This is not the case in Thailand, and in the difference, the nub of the difficulty is

23

exposed. With demand for new agricultural land in the tropics expected to remain at about 10 million hectares per year (FAO data tabulated in Sargent 1990b), and despite the politics of the global carbon budget, widespread establishment of 'simple' plantations (monocultures with a narrow purpose and uniform structure) in less developed and tropical countries is unlikely to be socially acceptable, economically sustainable or environmentally stable.

Ways forward

There are two ways forward: **either** plantations can be treated as crops in simple systems, and only established in a favourable economic climate on land without alternative claim (as in Sweden); or plantations can have a **complex** structure or purpose, by *de novo* design or by being grown within natural forest, as classical silviculture dictates. Thus for example, trees may be planted on catchments to promote growth of natural vegetation, or plantations might be designed to be intercropped, giving direct benefit to local farmers, or established within degrading forests, maintaining as much of the existing ecosystem processes as possible.

There is, of course, a third way: to manage, protect and use natural forest more wisely and effectively than at present.

Comparisons

The assumption that man-made forests are fully equivalent and exchangeable with natural forests is widely perpetuated. In preparing assessment of world forst cover, for example, FAO aggregates natural forest with timber plantations but, interestingly, not with plantations of rubber (which are now also used for timber), oil palm or other woody perennial crops (Tho 1991).

What are the diffences? What are the similarities? What is important? Of course, biological quality and social and financial values differ from forest to forest and plantation to plantation. Biological quality and social value are not unique properties of natural forest, nor is financial value a sole attribute of plantations.

It is clear that in weighing values there must be a standard. That standard is now recognized as sustainability. Although everyone has a concept of what sustainability means, a proper definition has become more and more tenuous as the word is juggled between scientists, philosophers, politicians and the press (categories within which all those concerned can surely identify themselves!). Jodha (1991; both scientist and philosopher) links sustainable human welfare with sustainable resource use. He deftly avoids definition. Instead, he describes **sustainable land use** as:

> a pattern or system of use, which can ensure flow of products and services from land to meet current, and, if needed, increasing levels of demand, without damaging its long-term production potential.

This is very general, but more exact definitions have been misleading. The particular problem with defining what is sustainable in a given situation is that the situation is very unlikely to remain constant. Within a given market, population or environment, it may be possible to predict the effect of particular impacts. But when all these variables are changing and interacting in ways about which we are at best uncertain, it is almost certainly impossible to know what the outcome will be. Thus it is essential to retain **resilience** and **flexibility** in the environment. In this lies the real difference between naturally-established and artificially-established resources.

A man-made forest has been selected and designed to maximize defined objectives – usually productivity and profit – under certain social, environmental and economic conditions. Selection, trial and experiment prescribe what grows optimally under conditions which exist in a particular locality at a particular time. A single genotype with structural and physiological uniformity may be chosen. This is a simple ecosystem. Being man-made, it is by definition disturbed, and tends to be unstable. The biological diversity which might confer stability under changing conditions has been sacrificed in the interest of uniform, mass production. And profit? What happens if the market changes, the population grows and demands more land, and the climate alters? Wherefore sustainability then?

At the other end of the spectrum, a natural forest is a diverse community of organisms interacting and competing for space and survival. It is extremely stable under most natural disturbances – young trees, often of very different species and growth habits, replacing old without destroying the integrity of the whole. Where the future is uncertain, there is an overwhelming importance in biological diversity. This diversity makes possible a spectrum of responses to change and competition strategies for differing circumstances, some or many of which are likely to be successful. Biological diversity leads to differences in biophysical function, generalized in the jargon as 'services', as well as in how the forest can be used and what it will produce – 'the goods'!

Services

Biodiversity

A plantation has low biodiversity. It is dominated by one or a few, often genetically uniform, tree species. The trees may be densely planted, or be managed so that no understorey exists. A tropical moist forest, on the other hand, is amongst the most diverse of ecosystems. In Cameroon the author recorded more than 200 named tree species in three one-hectare experimental plots. Fewer than 60 of those species were common to all three plots. In a plot of only 100 square metres at Las Horquetas in Costa Rica, 73 tree species and a total of 233 vascular plants were recorded (Palmer and Synnott, 1991, unpublished). This is called alpha diversity: the richness of species numbers within a community. Beta diversity refers to the rates at which species may replace one another in time. However, only in relation to gamma diversity, which reflects the relative uniqueness of a community within a landscape and the complexity of that landscape, can plantations sometimes justifiably vie with natural forests. Plantations are often of non-native species which may be very different from those of the surrounding environment – and hence plantations may have some gamma diversity value. Natural forest may, of course, be surrounded by rice paddies, and also have gamma diversity value!

Plantations are likely to increase in alpha diversity over time, although a closing canopy will reduce the ground flora. Animals will move into plantations, particularly for refuge and nesting habitat, if not for more specialized feeding niches. Evans and Wright (1988) have documented increases in numbers of animal species over a period of several years in the Usutu pine plantations in the highlands of Swaziland:

> The forest provides excellent cover for wildlife. The numbers and variety of animals have increased to include antelope and buck, monkeys, baboons, porcupines, antbears, bushbabies, warthogs, guinea-fowl, lynx, spring hares, rock rabbits, mongooses, honey badger,

cape fox, civet and cerval – animals uncommon in the adjacent highveldt.

Soil structure

Soil-building and maintenance processes are dependent on the soil flora and fauna. Plant litter (leaves, bark and wood) provides much of the organic material which is broken down by small vertebrates, invertebrates and micro-organisms and is mixed with weathered minerals to form soil. Clearly the relationships are complex, and a certain level of diversity is required to ensure that all materials are incorporated. Some organisms are indiscriminate in the materials they utilize. Others are specific – or have preferences. Anyone walking through a mixed woodland in Britain early in the year will note that oak (*Quercus* spp.) leaves are still abundant on the ground several months after having fallen from the trees. This is because earthworms (usually *Lumbricus* spp.) feed preferentially on leaves with less tannin, taking oak leaves only when alternatives are exhausted or fail.

Brunig and Schneider (1991, unpublished) have shown that the diversity of soil organisms is closely dependent on the microclimate of the forest floor. This microclimate is influenced by rates of interception and extinction of light, and also of water, nutrients and pollutants, and is therefore determined by the physical structure of the forest. Complex soil communities may occur in a plantation, although the relative structural uniformity of the plantation will reduce variability in microclimate, and hence in soil communities. Further, there may be effects of biological uniformity. For example, certain commonly grown plantation trees such as *Pinus* spp., have high levels of organic acids in their discarded leaves (needles) which inhibit the activity and limit the variety of soil micro-organisms. This leads to the development of an acid mor soil in which plant litter accumulates and decomposes only slowly. Mor soils are hospitable to a limited range of plants, and hence dependent animals and micro-organisms. With a limited spectrum of soil species, and with the intense nutrient demands of fast-growing plantation trees, the ecosystem may not produce sustainable volumes of timber without the use of fertilizers.

Erosion and hydrology

There are myths about the role of plantations in containing soil erosion. Trees are, of course, important for soil conservation, but irrespective of whether erosion occurs in sheets, through gulleys or through slumping, it is **diversity** of forest structure, and most particularly, the presence of an understorey and ground cover which are important in protecting the soil. In many circumstances, establishing grassland may be a better preventative strategy. Brunig *et al.* (1975) reported annual erosion rates in the range of 20–160 tons per hectare under densely-planted teak (*Tectona grandis*) with no understorey on moderate slopes. This compares unfavourably both with natural forest under comparable slope and climate conditions, at 0.2–10 tons per hectare, and with teak plantations with trees sufficiently widely spaced to enable development of a natural understorey, at 2–10 tons per hectare.

Leaf litter and humus are also critical in providing surface protection to the soil. Litter breaks the impact of water drops; humus promotes soil porosity and absorptive capacity. Where leaf litter from plantations is collected for fuel, there is little surface protection and a humic soil will not develop. In pulpwood plantations (*Eucalyptus* spp.) in Vietnam, for example, this has become a very severe problem (Sargent 1991).

In general, erosion is not dependent on the presence or absence of trees, but on the level of human disturbance. For example, traditional forms of shifting agriculture are not responsible for widespread erosion. It is the move away from rotational land management towards continuous use – or what has been dubbed 'shiftless' agriculture – that may cause massive downstream sedimentation (Hamilton and Pearce 1987). Plantations which are intensively managed, and from which diversity is weeded or excluded, will give rise to much higher rates of erosion than natural forest.

Biodiversity, as such, plays no role in flood control, although vegetation structure will both influence net transpiration and contribute to the porosity and water-holding capacity of the soil. On catchments which are tree-covered, rather than grass- or shrub-covered, there will be some reduction in overall and peak flow, but flooding will still occur once the soil's acceptance rate for water is exceeded. Where erosion and downstream sedimentation are severe, dams and other flood prevention mechanisms will be less effective; there is therefore benefit in less disturbed ecosystems, where erosion is likely to be less severe.

Neverthless, plantations may have a useful ameliorating effect on peak flows, although where there are downstream water shortage problems, the excess water transpiration of fast-growing plantations, such as those of *Eucalyptus camaldulensis*, is likely to be deleterious, reducing net flow and contributing to drought potential.

Greenwood, Klein and Beresford (1985) measured and compared

transpiration from grassland and two species of *Eucalyptus* and recorded average annual transpiration from grassland and *Eucalyptus* as 390 mm and 2700 mm respectively. Many species of *Eucalyptus* have extensive tap roots which enable them to thrive where the water table is low, and where other tree species may not survive. Studies in Karnataka, described in Kanowski and Savill (1990), suggest that plantations of *Eucalyptus tereticornis* and *Eucalyptus camaldulensis* are using no more water than degraded natural forest on adjacent sites. However, where water shortage is likely to be a problem, the benefits of fast-growing trees, which generally do transpire more water than slow- or low-growing vegetation, must be carefully weighed against water costs.

> Most ecological effects can only be evaluated with reference to what society wants. For example – is wood or water more important in a particular locality, or wood rather than grass fodder? High consumption of water is a characteristic to be valued if the purpose of planting is to dry out a swamp, but it is to be deprecated, and may rightly be criticized, if it draws down the water table in an area where water is in short supply or can be used for a highly profitable irrigated crop.
>
> (Poore and Fries 1985)

Climate

Trees moderate climate, especially at a very local or 'micro' level. Under the canopy of a forest, air speed is reduced, direct insolation is largely excluded, humidity is likely to increase, and fluctuations in temperature and humidity are diminished. There are many trees which develop preferentially in these sheltered conditions, and which are consequently difficult to bring into plantation. These include slow-growing tropical timber species, many of which are currently of very high value. There are other trees, pioneer species, which need more light, and which will tolerate greater extremes; these tend to be lower-value softwoods, but include many of the mahoganies (*Swietenia* spp.). Natural forests depend on the balance and interaction between these different kinds of trees. In a plantation, generally only trees with pioneer characteristics are grown. However attempts are being made, for example in Vietnam, to grow certain *Dipterocarps* – high forest hardwood species with much prized, uniform, timber – under nurse crops of trees such as *Acacia mangium*, which mimic natural forest conditions.

Climate influences the forest – dictating what will grow in it – but large areas of the forest itself may also have regional and global climatic effects, the precise influence and impacts of which are still controversial. At the regional level, transpiration will increase air humidity, which may contribute to increased rainfall. The reflectivity or albedo of a forest canopy is very different from that of bare ground; temperature and air turbulence will be lower; and dustiness will be reduced. In Ghana, for example, the increasing impact of the *Harmattan*, a dust-laden desert wind, on the southern coastal capital of Accra, is attributed to loss of forest in the north. The interactions of forests with the carbon balance and global warming have been discussed above.

Goods

Forest goods are those things which provide direct benefits to people, and are produced as a result of forest disturbance, use and management. These include timber and non-timber products, grazing and fallow. The fundamental difference between natural forest and plantations lies, as we have seen, in differences in biodiversity. Diversity also dictates the quality and quantity of goods provided. Where plantation biodiversity is relatively low, the range of goods and services from a plantation is largely dictated by the plantation design. Complex plantations may provide a broad range of benefits in addition to pulp or timber. These include local access for hunting, fuelwood, fruit harvesting, taungya and intercropping purposes. Plantations certainly provide some recreational value in the North, although there is little evidence to suggest that these have acquired the status which sacred groves have in the South! Nevertheless, the goods remain limited compared to natural forests. Even the more complex plantations are unlikely to provide for the full spectrum of needs of the poorest members of the community, especially women and children and particularly in times of seasonal hardship or catastrophe and where people are denied access. In such circumstances, and continually for autochthonous peoples, natural forests provide best for subsistence.

Where there is local access to natural forest, in many parts of the tropics income is greatly supplemented by trade in the forest's non-timber products. These products are diverse, and are traded mainly in local markets. Where a particular product has a wider market, and is traded nationally or internationally, higher demands for quality, uniformity and continuity in supply need to be met. In many cases, the solution has been to take such non-timber products into plantation production – or, where important drugs are concerned, to synthesize the active principle. Hence, except for those products such as Brazil nuts, where there are biological constraints (in this case absence of habitat for the pollinator) to growth in monoculture, most non-timber products from natural forest are important for local rather than mass markets.

The supply of mass markets requires commercial investment, which tends to remove control or interest from the local community. This reflects a general distinction between plantations and natural forest, in that the former tends to benefit fewer, and wealthier people, whilst the latter may contribute to the livelihoods of many, including those who exist outside the formal monetary and market structure.

Clearly, both in terms of goods and services, there is an important role for plantations – but this role must be defined in terms of economic, social and biological sustainability. Plantations should be established only within an appropriate land use context, once the economic, environmental and social implications have been considered and judged acceptable, and where there is adequately forecast demand. In Nepal (Griffin 1988) and Papua New Guinea (Sargent 1989), and many other parts of the world, commercial trees have been planted for which it is now recognized there is no market. And given the context of a rapidly reducing natural forest resource and changing climate scenario, plantations should not be established in place of prime natural forest.

Protection of natural forest

It is curious to note the very strong coincidence between loss of tropical forest and expansion of areas of tropical forest plantation (see above). This, at the most obvious level, calls into question the argument so widely perpetuated that the establishment of plantations serves to reduce the pressure for timber extraction from the natural forest, and hence protects the natural resource. What really happens is that competition from plantation-grown timber, by substitution, reduces the competitive advantage of most timber from the natural forest. The argument should follow that natural forest will not therefore be logged to the same extent. The reality is that when the natural forest has a less immediately realizable value to the concessionaire or logger, he will invest less in protection for continued production, and forests become diminished as alternative, more profitable, land uses take over. This occurs either at a formal, considered level, where land control resides with the state of concessionaire, or at an informal level where farmers or communities are able to establish farming claims in the forest.

Plantations are a complement to natural forest; they are not a substitute. At present, because intact natural forest has a relatively low perceived and realizable value, it is being lost. Many of the lands which now support uniform areas of fast-growing, sometimes alien, trees, have been converted from natural forest. In many areas of the tropics, natural forest management is not sustainable and resources are not protected, because it is difficult for those who hold direct reponsibility for the forest to fully anticipate and recognize the potential of second- or third-cycle logging returns. There are clear needs to demonstrate the long-term benefits of good natural forest management and to show that there are substantial profits to be made over time.

Many forest policies focus strongly on capturing natural forest rent for national purposes, as opposed to local purposes. However, where the realizable value of the resource to the local community or concessionaire is low, there may be little interest in protecting the resource, or in good management. Policies which have been based on increasing the cost of extraction (through stumpage or royalties) and reducing the margin of profitability (through export, value added and sales taxes) to the concessionaire irrespective of the quality of management, may be misplaced, as may policies which neglect the interests of local people. Under this, which is the current scenario through much of the tropical world, forests are being lost through mismanagement and encroachment. Policies should seek to place the highest possible value on forest resources which are presently moving towards extinction, and the highest possible return for good management and protection of forest lands.

Plantations have been used to create buffer zones around natural forest. The physical barrier provided by these often carefully protected areas of planted trees may well be locally important. However, plantations seldom if ever substitute for all those goods and services for which local populations depend on the natural forest, and there have been relatively few effective examples (Sayer 1991).

The problem of increasing the value of natural forest is quite distinct from the question of physical protection by plantation buffer zones. The latter concerns local negotiations regarding access and use rights, and compensation where these cannot be assured. The former is a matter of economic and land-use policy, and is linked in particular to the market price of wood and wood products; and to the need for policy recognition and valuation of the social, cultural and environmental benefits of natural forests. The most urgent need is for natural forests and plantations to be considered as separate – though related – entities in policy. Only then will policy ambiguity about their substitutability be removed, and incidences of unwarranted deforestation to create plantations be curtailed.

However, in promoting plantations, whilst it is recognized that products are produced which, with effective policy and good land-use and economic planning, will reduce pressure on the natural forest, such circumstances are infrequent and potentially deleterious effects must also be taken into account.

Choices

In general, the more diverse the forest, the more secure the services and the wider the range of goods. However, the full range of goods may not be deliverable cost-effectively using current techniques, and so human intervention will tend to reduce biodiversity and yield a narrower range of benefits in favour of larger volumes.

Moreover, those who manage the forest for industrial purposes are likely to make a deliberate decision to select a simple system. It is much easier and generally more profitable (given that environmental benefits are seldom valued in the market place) to grow a crop with one or two species, where growth rates and responses to environmental variability can be predicted, than to deal with the complex ecology of a natural forest.

It has been shown that the move towards plantations in the tropics has been stimulated by the increasing scarcity and value of the natural resource – to the point where investment in growing trees *de novo* has become a realistic option.

If we conclude that there is no real evidence that plantations protect natural forest, and, indeed, that by providing alternative sources of uniform and relatively cheap timber, they may detract from the value that can be attributed to a forest managed for timber, under what circumstances should plantations be established?

Although plantations can be established:

in place of existing closed forest; in place of other natural vegetation such as savanna, scrub or grassland; on degraded or waste land either as a potential crop or to assist in the control of erosion; within agricultural land, as shelter belts, part of agroforestry systems, or as intensively managed crops for wood production

(Poore and Fries 1985)

they are only successful where species and site selection is right, where there is no ownership conflict, and where the rights and interests of all concerned are taken fully into account. The location and boundaries of plantations must therefore respond to environmental conditions and to the needs and customs of the local communities. Plantations must not be perceived as a strategy for state or corporation control or ownership of land.

There are four interests with which the establishment of plantations should primarily be concerned. The Government, representing the people at large and interpreting global concerns; industry, providing the investment funds and seeking profit; the local community, with rights, interests and often compelling needs; and the environment, with which we are most concerned in this chapter on choices between natural forest and plantation.

In deciding where a plantation should be established, all these interests must be taken into account. Plantations should be grown within a context of:

Government:
• Political stability
• Good land-use planning
• Forest policy which gives distinct – but coordinated – attention to the separate matters of the value of natural forests, the importance of the local community, and industrial demands for timber

Industry:
• Predictable demand for plantation products
• Adequate investment and planning capacity
• Proximity to market and adequate infrastructure

Community:
• Clearly defined land and tree tenure
• Equitable attention to the multiple needs of the local community, and local involvement in decision making, management and profits

Environment:
• Adequate attention to the value, protection and management of natural forest
• Attention to local and global environmental concerns
• Attention to species and site selection

The growth of plantations with multiple purposes, or where certain common property rights can be protected or established, provides potential for compromise between different interests.

In Côte d'Ivoire, a study was made of various silvicultural regimes, from minor intervention in natural forests, to industrial plantation establishment. The project covered 1,200 hectares at three sites within the three principal ecological zones of the moist forest:

> After ten years of regular measurement, it is clear that the management of natural forest can be justified from an economic point of view, since the ratio of extra commercial value produced to costs is of the same magnitude or greater than that of forest plantations set up in the same area. Over thirty years estimations (predictions) are about one extra cubic metre produced for every US$ 5.60 invested in the treatment of natural forest, and for plantations of high quality hardwood about US$ 7.40 invested per cubic metre produced.
> (Mengin-Lecreux and Durand 1987)

This work is often cited to indicate the potential value and productivity of natural forest management versus plantations (e.g. Rietbergen quoted in Kanowski and Savill 1991). What it has really done, however, is to compare returns from planting within natural forest (classical silviculture) with those from planting in monoculture on cleared land (the work provides no strict comparison with logging from natural forest). In this case, both modern and classical planting options are viable. Theoretical models, comparing returns from a plantation intercropped by local farmers with those from monocultures, indicate the viability of intercropping under certain conditions (Sargent 1991). In both these comparisons, additional social or environmental benefits are guaranteed by the more complex (non-monoculture) strategy.

Questions of the sustainability of natural forest management are raised where silvicultural activities (line or enrichment planting, poison girdling etc.) are intensive. However, considerable biodiversity is preserved compared to clear felling and establishment of plantation *de novo*. Available data relating to natural forest cover do not distinguish forest which has been severely altered by silvicultural manipulation, although, because investment in such forest has been higher, it is more likely to be protected than forest which has been logged and left.

Changing economic demands and pressures, and developing environmental and social awareness, provide a complex and constantly moving stage, upon which judgements and predictions about establishing plantations may not always be easy. Given the lack of absolute knowledge and our diffuse understanding of the future, particularly in terms of climate change and the resulting fragility of genetically simple systems or monocultures, plantations must be made more diverse, robust and resilient, whilst retaining their primary function, be it wood production or land reclamation.

Conclusions

1. The choice about whether and where to establish plantations should be about the best use of land within local political, economic, social and environmental contexts. In practice, it has more often been about who controls and owns the land.
2. It is mistaken to assume that plantations substitute directly for natural forests. In natural forests, biological diversity confers resilience and stability, and provides multiple benefits for local communities – particularly in times of seasonal stress and catastrophe. Such resilience is, in contrast, minimal in industrial plantations.
3. Industrial plantations, on the other hand, are complementary to natural forest, in much the same way as agriculture is. They are artificial agricultural systems, requiring major inputs and investment. Where biomass productivity is the principal purpose for which they are grown, they are intentionally unstable. They can, however, be structured to provide certain additional social, biological and environmental benefits. Unlike natural forest, the biomass productivity and management impacts of plantations are relatively easy to predict.
4. There is a continuum between undisturbed natural forest and completely artificial forest, which is reflected in the continuum from many different benefits towards few uniform benefits. Silvicultural activities within natural forests tend to lead towards a simple, predictable, plantation-like state, in which resilience may be lowered.
5. Where inputs are lowered, plantations will generally move towards a more natural (diverse) state. They can therefore assist land restoration and rehabilitation, and provide certain catchment functions.
6. Given conflicting social and agricultural needs, the establishment of carbonforest (plantation designed for carbon sequestering purposes) in the tropics at rates promoted by the Noordwijk Convention will not be possible. Strategies to increase carbon sequestration should focus on the

wise use and protection of natural forest, and on encouraging tree growth within the agricultural landscape.

7. Except under very specific circumstances, plantations have not contributed to the protection of natural forests. Rather, because plantations have a higher perceived and realizable value than natural forest, plantation growth has contributed to loss of the natural resource, and plantations themselves have been established by removing natural forest. Protection of natural forest can be achieved only when policies and practices lead to an increased value in relation to alternative land uses, including agriculture and plantation.

8. Increasing world demands for wood cannot be met from natural forest alone. Natural forest should be harvested for high quality and decorative timbers and for multiple local goods. Plantations are needed to provide industrial wood and cellulose.

9. If plantations are to be established on land where there are competing needs, rights and interests, complex solutions may need to be found. These involve increasing biological diversity to provide increasing stability and more varied goods and services, and improving access through strategies giving common property or individual rights to defined components of the resource.

There is therefore not a choice to be made between natural forest and plantation, but rather a realization that they should be additive and supportive. The revised World Conservation Strategy, *Caring for the Earth: A Strategy for Sustainable Living* (IUCN, UNEP, WWF 1991) states clearly that:

> plantations should be in addition to natural and modified forest; they should not replace them.

To achieve this, it is critical to ensure that the establishment of plantations does not, by competition, detract from the realizable and recognized values of natural forests on which their continued survival depends.

Only when the distinctions between plantations and natural forests are clearly recognized by those who influence policy making and planning, can rational forest land use – based on the integration and prioritization of attributes and benefits under particular circumstances – be achieved.

Box 2.1
Economic transitions towards forest plantations

Neoclassical economists have assumed that such factors as natural resources, capital and labour are substitutable, so that shortages in one do not significantly limit the productivity of the other. If one factor becomes scarce, its price will rise. This will provide incentives to exploit marginal stocks more efficiently, to develop cost-effective substitutes, and to conserve the use of existing supplies by curbing demand. Technological innovation has assisted this dynamic process.

Hyde and Seve (1991) studied this economic transition mechanism in the case of Malawi's natural and plantation forests. Fuelwood was assumed to be the only product of forestry. The total supply of fuelwood (MCst) was assumed to be composed of the supply of fuelwood from indigenous natural forests (MCit) and the supply from exogenous plantation forests (MCe). The intersection of the total supply and the demand (Dt) indicates the market price of fuelwood (Pt) in year t. When, during n years, the demand is shifted from Dt into Dt+n, all accessible natural forests (MCit+n) are depleted. Hence, the shifted demand (Dt+n) and only the supply from the forest plantations (MCe) govern the new price (Pt+n).

However, most of the goods and services of tropical forests lack *in situ* markets and prices and, consequently, economic transition mechanisms do not operate efficiently under tropical circumstances. Even where

---

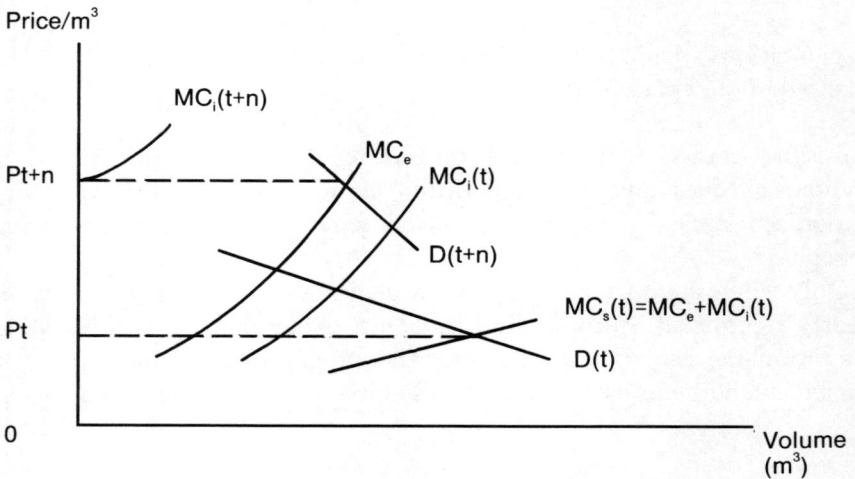

markets for fuelwood work in cities and on roadsides, they are missing in forests *in situ*. Hence increasing relative scarcities of fuelwood are not, in fact, reflected in higher stumpage prices. Subsequently, deforestation of natural forests in Malawi and similar cases has a tendency to advance faster and further than under efficiently functioning markets.
Matti Palo
Source: Hyde, W.F. and J.E. Seve, *Malawi: A rapid economic appraisal of smallholders' response to severe deforestation* (1991) [for full citation see 'References'].

Box 2.2
Complex plantations

There are four principal elements of complexity in plantations. These relate to landscape, species composition, management and ownership:

Landscape: Plantations should be planned to minimize impact on the landscape. This can be done by creating many individually homogeneous planting units within the plantation, whose boundaries, roads and fire breaks should follow or reflect natural changes in vegetation, slope, soil type or drainage. Generally, boundaries should be buffered with native planting for conservation of the physical and biological environment. Where natural forest exists, this should be preserved.

Multiple species: The use of many species can increase profitability and social acceptability, by more effective use of the available space (vertically as well as land area) and by sharing the varied benefits. In certain *Dipterocarp* forests, for example, it has been shown that fruit trees are most common in the understorey, substantially avoiding competition for space with timber trees, and also providing valuable products for local people. More generally, mixtures of species with a broad genetic base provide insurance against unpredicted events, although they are likely to be more difficult to manage than single-species plantations.

Agroforestry management: There are particular environmental, social and financial benefits to be gained from managing a plantation with an annual intercrop (agroforestry) system. These include:

• continuous annual income for participating farmers
• sharing of costs of plantation maintenance with agricultural enterprises

- little, if any, reduction in wood volume production
- intensified land use and productivity
- synergistic effects of agricultural and tree crops (although some of these can be negative)
- improved wildlife habitat
- reduced risk of accidental or deliberate burning through:
— increased spacing
— reduced occurrence of grass-burning hazard
— increased responsibility of farmers with intercrops

Land-holding: A balance should be drawn between lands held by the plantation investor and those held by the rural population. On land held by the investor, planning and management can be optimized for environmental benefit. On land held by the rural population, social satisfaction is likely to be greatest.

C.S.

Principal source: Sargent, C., *The Khun Song Plantation Project. A socio-economic and environmental analysis and recommendations towards the establishment and management of a plantation in Chantaburi Province by Shell Companies of Thailand* (London: IIED, 1990).

CHAPTER 3

BUILDING FROM THE PAST: FOREST PLANTATIONS IN HISTORY

Stephen M.J. Bass

Introduction

Historical factors have shaped the purpose, location, extent and composition of all forests. In turn, forests and forest products – notably wood – have been key in the development of civilizations (Perlin 1989).

Foresters are good at looking to the future. Indeed, early economic techniques for dealing with future costs and revenues were contributed by foresters. Yet forestry decisions remain based on analyses of the present situation and forecasts of the future, in relative ignorance of the past. Materials and skills in forest history are lacking, and forest policy hence develops on ground that is not as rich as it could be.

The historical roles of wild forests – as opposed to plantations – in providing raw materials for industry and empire have been examined in some economic and colonial histories. There is, in fact, a current fashion for historical studies of the use and transformation of tropical forests (e.g. Tucker and Richards 1983). These studies demonstrate that, over the last two centuries, tropical forests have been overexploited, principally for strategic and economic purposes (Evans 1982), and in recent decades the rate of deforestation has escalated. As natural forests have declined, planted trees have become increasingly important in the ladscape (Romm 1991). Yet, so far, there has been little historical work examining the reasons for tree planting.

Plantation histories might better explain today's plantation legacy. At the most mundane level, good historical records may help in avoiding the repetition of past technical failures. Had Daniel Ludwig examined the early literature on *Gmelina* in Burma, many of his hugely expensive mistakes in the Jari plantation, in Brazil, might have been avoided. At a more rarified level, historical studies of the sea change from forest liquidation to tree planting may reveal insights into evolving relationships with nature.

Forces shaping plantations in history

Environmental factors are clearly fundamental to shaping plantations and their impacts on society. When terrain, soil and water conditions constrain the availability and productivity of natural forests, plantations are favoured. Such conditions will also determine which plantation species can grow, and how well they will grow.

Except over the very long term and where they are affected by human activities, however, environmental factors are relatively constant. For this reason, and because the book predominantly addresses socio-political issues, this chapter concentrates on the **human factors** shaping plantations. Further, although the book focuses on tropical industrial plantations, many of the forces behind these plantations derive from the prevalent approaches to development of temperate countries. Hence a wider historical background, encompassing temperate as well as tropical countries, is offered in this chapter.

Politics and social factors

Dominant power structures – chieftainly, colonial, democratic, religious, economic, managerial – have been of overriding significance in dealing with scarcities of forest products and services. The extremes of colonial slavery and independent democracy have both resulted in vast plantations. The many different forms of social order witnessed over history have also been reflected in the type of plantation layout and management.

Early examples of organized forest protection and plantation were in favour of the ruling classes, often for private hunting reserves for royalty and other leaders. In the seventh century BC, the Persian King Khosrov II planted a forest for hunting, and built a palace within it. English Royal Forests were reserved for hunting and, in 1306, Edward I of England reserved all the oak in the Royal forest for use of the Crown (Adlard 1992). Such forest reservation and afforestation diminished the common man's access to forests. Local conflicts ensued and, as a result, forest use (usufruct) rights became established or tree plantations outside the reserves were established by local people.

In this century, the patronage of forest plantations by royalty and religious leaders has given way to leadership by the state and, increasingly, by corporations, aid agencies and local communities.

Stability in society, politics and the economy has invariably been essential for plantation forestry, which by nature is a long-term enterprise. The termination of political and social conflicts has often provided the impetus for major afforestation. In times of war, forests have been exploited for building ships, and for fuel; and enemy forests have been ravaged. In turn, in times of peace, plantations have been established to replenish losses and to create future strategic reserves.

Legislation has occasionally been passed to require planting. Yet, except where it has been backed up with incentives, it has rarely been effective. For example, in late seventeenth-century France, legislation was passed obliging landowners to plant five per cent of their land; but in most provinces this met with insuperable resistance.

Cultural factors

Culture mediates between people and their local environment. The dominant force in cultural evolution was once the environment: now it is the decisions of man. Decisions are increasingly being made at national and global levels, imposing a growing uniformity of (Western) culture throughout the world.

The cultures of the world lie on many points between the extremes of dominance over nature and subjugation to nature. In the historical development of the West, a cultural sequence can be traced from forests treated as adversary, to forests treated as refuge, then as factory, and ultimately as pleasure-ground (see e.g. Adlard 1992). Western cultures can be said to have evolved away from the forest, treating the forest in a detached, instrumentalist manner. Natural forest management and afforestation have been introduced only in the 'later' stages, when there are economic imperatives for managing and increasing forest wealth, and adequate social and political stability to make this practicable.

These various perceptions of forests occur in other cultures, but not necessarily within a sequence comparable to that of the West. Many non-Western cultures remain rooted in the forest. Hence there can be considerable clashes between cultural approaches to forests in periods of major transition – e.g. as empires and industry grow and as cultures meet. The introduction of Western scientific forestry and plantations to India has been said to have 'weeded out' the diversity of both trees and people; uniform monocultures of plants and people are managed externally whereas, in contrast, the survival of local tropical forests has depended on the survival of human societies modelled on the forest (Shiva and Bandyopadhyay in Head and Heinzman 1990).

The cultural predisposition to create boundaries, and the ability to defend them against other social groups and environmental factors, are fundamental to a society's predisposition, or otherwise, to create tree plantations. Belief systems may be said to exist to delineate, clarify and reinforce boundaries: of pure and polluted, of accepted and taboo, and of natural and domesticated (Weiskel 1983). Western cultures tend to seek clear, utilitarian boundaries between simplified areas of land use – a tree plantation and a wheat field, for example. Partly as a result, the Western imperative to create distinct, simple blocks of plantation is great.

Other cultures do not draw such distinct boundaries between the natural and the domesticated, however. Forest gardens and swidden systems of annual and perennial crops and trees in intimate, apparently boundaryless mixes – the kinds of mix which Western obervers characterize as 'untidy' – represent an incredibly rich cultural heritage.

Cultural attitudes, movements and fashions have changed most rapidly in the last twenty years, with the spread of Western 'consumer' lifestyles. Underlying such lifestyles is the belief that consumption and wealth accumulation is desirable. This has had immediate implications for the consumption of wood, which has tended to increase with development: in industrialized countries today, the consumption per person of all major forest products is now three and a half times that of someone in a developing country (Arnold 1991a). Yet there is now emerging an anti-materialistic culture, one which is finding expression in the market place (ironically) in the demand for 'green' products.

Financial and economic factors

Plantations may be established if demands for forest products and services are rising and supplies from natural forest sources are decreasing. Where the marginal cost of production from natural forests exceeds the marginal cost of products from plantations, the latter will tend to be favoured.

The ways in which forests and forest products have been valued have therefore influenced investment in plantations relative to natural forests. The prevalent undervaluing of natural tropical forests in recent history has acted as a disincentive for planting, and an incentive for liquidating natural forests.

In the last few decades, virtually all forest products have become scarcer and most markets have become monetized. The financial imperative for forest plantations has become dominant, and has led to a great rise in private plantation investment. The intimate economic linkages of wood-using industries at the global level, and the strong dependence of

plantation economics upon industrial economics, now means that industrial plantations as far apart as Brazil and Australia are in competition
(Dargavel and Kengen 1992).

Science and technology

Three technological phases can be defined by their prevalent energy use:
wood energy (much of Africa, for example, is still in this era), coal and
steam (many large developing countries, such as India and China), and
petroleum and electricity (the West and many other countries). Some
countries simultaneously experience all three. Only in the latter phase,
however, have technological forces generally favoured plantations over
natural forests.

In the **wood energy phase**, wood is both the fundamental energy source
and the main material resource, because it is abundant. Only in very
localized instances of severe wood shortages are plantations established.
In general, shortages are met by importing natural forest wood, or by
moving to other energy supplies – notably coal, the next phase.

In the **coal and steam phase**, wood provides both the infrastructure to
mine coal (pit props, etc.) and the infrastructure to use coal (railway
wagons and factories). The more specific technological requirements of
this phase demand wood inputs of a more uniform specification. Such
demands tend to favour plantation products over natural forest products,
yet labour remains cheap enough to convert natural forest products to the
required specification, and technological tolerances are still large enough
to accept minimally converted natural forest products. This delays the
establishment of plantations.

It is the technological demands of the **petroleum and electricity phase**
that have led, finally, to the ascendancy of plantations. Wood continues to
provide a major construction material but is also of value for its cellulose,
used in various industrial processes, notably the manufacture of paper.
Mass production and transport processes to feed large and specific
markets require huge, reliable and cheap supplies of uniform forest
products, which are better provided from plantations than from natural
forests. This is especially the case for the paper industry, which has
spawned large monocultural plantations all over the world.

The petroleum/electricity phase has also brought about a range of
technological developments which have altered the shape and management of plantations:

• mechanization

- pesticides and herbicides
- genetics, breeding and biotechnology
- silviculture
- forest physiology and ecology
- wood/paper technology

Historical roles of plantations

The earliest roles of tree plantations

Tree planting for material needs has evolved in two ways: through manipulating natural forest in swidden; and through clearing land as part of settled agriculture. Trade in forest products, and the need to ameliorate the environmental problems of settled agriculture, have both fostered further plantation developments. From the earliest times, tree planting has also been carried out for religious and aesthetic reasons.

Swidden, and tree planting within natural forests

For several thousand years, forest-based civilizations have nurtured tree groves within natural forests. A classic example is the 'home garden' of the Kayapo in Brazilian rain forest. The Kayapo collect many forest species and concentrate them in complex groves of mixed planted and naturally-occurring species within the natural forest, selectively cutting back unwanted species. Each type of home garden – 'friends who grow together', as the Kayapo call them – has its own management regime for producing timber, other fibres, food and medicine. The concern today is that there is no longer the social and cultural stability required for maintaining home gardens (Clay 1988).

Tree planting in settled agriculture

In the earliest settled agriculture, semi-domesticated grain fields were separate from dwellings. Gradually, the skills of cultivation were developed; and this meant that dwellings and fields could be located together in villages – obviating the need for food caches and long-distance transport, which was burdensome before the draught animal or the wheel (Tannahill 1988).

By the neolithic age, the axe was widespread, and the consequent wholesale removal of trees and their replacement with annual crops necessitated social protection for valued natural forests and trees, through myth and religion. It also encouraged planting of selected trees on land that had been cleared – employing and adapting the plant selection and cultivation techniques of agriculture. By the sixth millennium BC, pistachio and almond cultivation had begun in Iran; and the olive was being spread around the shores of the Mediterranean from its native Syria and Anatolia, eased by vegetative propagation (Huxley 1978). The olive crop fed expanding states, and great importance was attached to the cultivation of the best varieties. Many other trees were cultivated for their oil: pine nut in China, walnut in Greece, and coconut in Asia. The network of irrigation canals which was developed in Mesopotamia provided ideal conditions for poplars and date palms, the trees clinging to the banks. So productive were the dates that they became the cheapest staples (Tannahill 1988).

Once crops and trees were being cultivated together, societies experienced profound political changes. The question of ownership of cultivated land became significant; cultivation changed the division of labour. Women took up the burden not only of the home and family but also of the fields and trees. Men were relieved of the burden of securing food through hunting; civic life developed and ambitions of military conquest were aroused (Tannahill 1988).

Plantations were an integral part of Roman estate management by the early second century BC, when Cato listed the profitable crops:

> Vines bring the greatest profit; next comes the irrigated garden; third the willow-bed; fourth the olive; fifth the meadow; sixth grain; seventh coppice wood; eighth orchard; ninth mast-wood . . . Plant elms and poplars round the borders of the farm and along the roads to give you leaves for the sheep and cattle, and timber when you need it.
>
> (From Meiggs 1982, quoted in Adlard 1992)

Virgil similarly exhorted farmers to plant trees locally, because transporting wood from increasingly far-off natural forests was slow, and environmental protection was necessary.

As ancient societies migrated and colonized, they brought the seeds, roots, bulbs and cuttings of their favoured species with them. The Romans spread olives, figs and vines all over the Mediterranean; they brought firs, stone pines, walnuts, figs, mulberries, cherries, plums and medlars to the British Isles (Wilkinson 1978). Trade also developed as people migrated and realized that certain species occurred, or grew better, in certain places. From early times in the Middle East, ever-increasing numbers of caravans carried high-value produce and seed, although they rarely carried plants (Huxley 1978). By 1500, the movement of seed sources for agricultural and tree crops had become truly global. However, timber trade was highly localized, constrained by transport. With the full development of the industrial empires of Europe, however, the movement of timber, and then of timber seed sources, was also to become global.

Early religious, aesthetic and cultural purposes for tree planting

With agricultural settlement, forest protection and tree planting became established in religious canon and myth. Ancient Chinese gardeners were watched over by a God of Planted Trees. Sylvanus, the Roman forest god, minded the work of clearing land in wooded country, and his province extended into the planting and care of trees (New Larousse 1968). Ancient sacred groves in Persia formed the source of planting material, once tree cultivation for material purposes had become widespread. (Sacred groves are still used as seed sources for plantation development in Africa, Latin America and Asia.)

From early times, planting for pleasure accompanied planting for material purposes. An ancient Chinese proverb tells 'when you have two pennies left in the world, buy a loaf of bread with one, and a lily with the other'. The first pleasure gardens were planted near the Tigris and Euphrates, inspired by the contemplation and idealization of the seemingly miraculous effects of irrigation on a barren landscape. Trees within them became objects of veneration (Jellicoe and Jellicoe 1975).

Trees were planted to indulge the passions of the ruling classes. The first recorded plant collecting expedition was for the frankincense trees *Boswellia carteri*: Queen Hatsepshut of Egypt had thirty-two trees brought by boat in 1482 BC from the Land of Punt (Somaliland) (Huxley 1978). With the domestication of the horse from 3000 BC in Central Asia came the first hunting park, and the first expansion of the planted landscape from the garden into the 'wild' environment. The middle eastern hunting park was laid out geometrically with planted trees, often obtained from far-off sources, and wild animals were introduced (Jellicoe and Jellicoe 1975). Under the Persians and others, plantations for aristocratic pleasure took on extreme proportions. At the end of the thirteenth century, Marco Polo observed that:

> The Great Khan has had made an earthwork . . . fully 100 paces in
> height and over a mile in circumference. This mound is covered with
> a dense growth of trees, all evergreens that never shed their leaves.
> And I assure you that whenever the Great Khan hears tell of a

particularly fine tree he has it pulled up, roots and all and with a quantity of earth, and transported to this mound by elephants . . . In this way he has assembled here the finest trees in the world. . .

Latham (translator)

Such ambitious planting was not entirely for the Great Khan's contemplation, however:

Along the main highways he has ordered trees to be planted on both sides, two paces distant from one another . . . For you will find these wayside trees in the heart of the wilderness; and a great boon they are to travellers and traders. They extend throughout every province and every kingdom . . . Besides the reasons already mentioned, he is all the more willing to have these trees planted because his soothsayers and astrologers declare that he who causes trees to be planted lives long.

Latham (translator)

Trees have been planted to demonstrate a landowner's or a state's power. The gardens of Roman villas were decisive extensions of anthropocentric architecture, and eventually Rome itself became a city of forested parks extending along the Tiber. In the expansion of French and some German and Italian estates – and later cities – in the sixteenth and seventeeth centuries, tree plantations extended into the surrounding landscape, the forms of these plantations extending the geometry and meaning of the architecture. In seventeenth century Moghul India, Agra was linked along the 400 miles to Lahore by a great avenue of chenar (oriental plane trees).

Some tree species have been planted for ornamental purposes for so long that wild specimens have never been seen, such as the Maidenhair tree *Ginkgo biloba*, domesticated in temples and gardens by the Chinese. Other common ornamental trees are rarely seen in the wild: the flamboyant *Delonix regia*, so widespread in tropical cities, has been seen only in one part of Madagascar; and the *Amherstia* has been seen only two or three times in the wild, all plants in cultivation originating from one specimen in a Burmese monastery

The politics of plantations in industrial development: the early example of England

England provides perhaps the best-documented illustration of how an industrialized country has evolved land-use patterns in which forest plantations are integral. The major influences in this evolution have been:

- land enclosure and land rights
- industrial and urban wood markets
- strategic and military requirements for timber
- official incentives for planting
- aesthetic values and clashes
- the material expression of power
- growing imperatives for environmental protection

These are examined in turn.

Land ownership and enclosure: from wild forests to hedgerows and small plantations

> Ye banish'd trees, ye make me deeply sigh
> Inclosure came, and all your glories fell.

(John Clare)

Field enclosure, principally for agriculture, began in the mid-fifteenth century, and resulted in widespread deforestation. It also excluded the poor and landless from forests, which ensured that wood became a market commodity. This ensured a tidy, early profit for the enclosing landowners. Once cleared for profit, however, forest lands were more valuable for agriculture than for reforestation and so, after an initial boom, timber supplies dwindled. Nevertheless, millions of miles of hedgerows were planted to mark the new boundaries, timber trees were grown within them, and strategically sited, small, geometrical 'covers' were planted for harbouring foxes for the hunt (Hoskins 1955). This planting was done by large landowners; it was possible for the common man only after 1756, when an Act provided for the enclosure of commons to plant trees (James 1981).

Incentives: patronage, publications, promotion and prizes

The major shift from forest protection to tree planting took off after the Commonwealth (1649–1660). During the Civil War, the weak system of managing and administering Royal forests, and the forests themselves, had practically disintegrated, being subject to abuse by all-comers. With the restoration of the monarchy, a yearning had developed for the restoration of England's woodlands (Perlin 1989). Following various petitions to the King, a Royal Society report was prepared. The author was John Evelyn, a Surrey landowner who was to become the strongest influence for tree planting in England.

In 1664, Evelyn published his seminal *Sylva or a Discourse of Forest*

Trees. Evelyn's politics were clear. He raged at the leaders and supporters of the Commonwealth for destroying 'all those many goodly woods and forests, which our more prudent ancestors left standing for the ornament and service of their country'; and insisted that 'nothing less than an universal [planting] of all sorts of trees will supply and well counter the defect'. The fear of naval invasion was evoked to persuade the influential to plant trees. Whereas earlier books had gone little further than discussing the politics of wood supply, Sylva was the first to add details on raising trees and producing timber.

Evelyn recommended block plantations, avenues and hedgerows, as well as coppice, and gave advice on the choice and tending of many species. At the time of the first edition of Sylva, most 'afforestation' involved seeding acorns and beech mast in the forest, on which Evelyn gave appropriate guidance. Yet soon it was found that transplants from nurseries were more successful, and his second edition discussed 'The Seminary' or nursery – which was subsequently to become increasingly popular (James 1981).

In his second edition, Evelyn could boast that 'millions of trees' had been planted by private landowners largely for profit, but also for patriotic reasons. Profit could be very high – in the Napoleonic Wars, unprecedented sums were paid for large oak and walnut (Hoskins 1955).

Other plantation protagonists, such as Batty Langley in his *Sure Method of Improving Estates by plantation of oak, elm, ash, beech and other timber trees* (1728), sought to increase the profitability of planting. And, from 1758, planting on a grand scale was encouraged by the Royal Society of Arts, which offered medals for meritorious plantations. For example, a Mr Congreve of Aldermaston planted 684,560 larch and sowed 73 acres to acorns from 1808 to 1811, winning two gold medals for his efforts. Such accelerated efforts encouraged the spread of numerous technical improvements – notably in nurseries. By the early nineteenth century, planting was no longer confined to a few enthusiasts. The Board of Agriculture's survey of farms and forests (from 1808 to 1817) noted that planting, rather than coppicing, was increasing in many counties, and told of the considerable superiority of private forests over Royal forests (James 1981).

Much of this planting was on open land. In contrast, in the management of existing forests, planting was considered to be but one of many forest regeneration techniques. The general aim was to secure natural regeneration through manipulating the mature forest's canopy and controlling felling coupes. Clear-felling, followed by planting, was only an emergency treatment for restoring degraded areas within forests. However, when it was applied widely in Saxony and Switzerland in the early nineteenth century, it led to the Norway spruce *Picea abies* dominating native beech and silver fir forests. The higher, earlier returns from the even-aged exotic spruce encouraged further planting, and was advocated by Cotta in his 'Anweisung zum Waldbau' (Silvicultural Methods) of 1816, which was influential in promoting plantations within Europe.

Tree planting for industry

Between the seventeenth and eighteenth centuries, there were sharp conflicts of opinion on forestry priorities in England. Some argued that industry had the principal claim on forests. Equally strong, localized lobbies argued for people's domestic needs, complaining that industry had driven wood prices too high. The Navy and others stressed the need for timber to maintain naval preparedness.

From the Elizabethan era, demands for wood – for fuel, tools, machinery, transport and infrastructure – increased greatly with the development of industries and with increasing affluence. This led to localized, but often severe, wood shortages. By the sixteenth century, the glass-making, clothing and especially iron-smelting industries required large amounts of fuelwood. Iron masters needed charcoal so badly that they would pay almost any price for it. A Lancashire iron manufacturer, finding 'no oak to be had in this country', paid highly to import charcoal from Scotland, despite its regularly turning to dust on the long journey (Perlin 1989).

Industry began to compete for wood with ordinary people, albeit increasingly affluent people. Householders no longer wished to build with inexpensive woods such as willow, but preferred oak. While some could afford the rising prices of construction wood, the poor often could not pay for firewood; after an iron works was built near Brighton in the 1550s, firewood prices rose by 400 per cent in 30 years (Perlin 1989).

Adverse public reaction precipitated much local legislation. In the sixteenth century, prospective iron founders in the Weald were forbidden to build foundries without also providing wood grown on their own land (Perlin 1989). Hence plantations and coppice came to be established by a good number of successful founders:

The iron industry, although initially leading to much destruction of woodland, had in the end the opposite effect, by providing a stimulus to the regular cultivation of coppice for charcoal.

(Thomas 1983)

However, the iron manufacturers' energy problems were not to be resolved mainly by tree planting, or even by the ability to travel further afield for natural forest wood, but rather by technology change. The price of capital in the rapidly-industrializing economy was too high to justify long-term investments in plantations. Rather investment in technology changes brought the greatest increases in production in the shortest periods. Manufacturers introduced processes and machinery that used fuelwood more efficiently. And, finally, they turned to coal. Their legacy of coppice was, in the end, not to be used for iron. Similar situations have arisen recently in the tropics, where large fuelwood plantations are established to deal with energy problems, ignorant of trends towards alternative energy technologies.

The net effect of three centuries of deforestation for industrial fuel and timber was observed by Maury in 1850. He wrote that deforestation in Great Britain had become so complete that

(She) is one of the countries with least forest in the world. Having destroyed the tree cover that protects the soil, she now excavates underground and consumes the fossil debris of the former forests that once covered the land.

(Maury 1850, quoted in Adlard 1992)

Tree planting for strategic and military purposes

We have noted the competing demands of industry, the domestic sector, and the Navy. The argument for Naval preparedness was to prove irresistible, and had the strongest influence in formal forest policy and legislation (Perlin 1989). James suggests, however, that despite the conflicts between the pro-industry lobby and those who favoured the Navy, the two did not compete in practice; for iron foundries took the small underwood, and the Navy the large timber (James 1981).

In the sixteenth and seventeenth centuries, major naval campaigns had resulted in widespread deforestation. Ship-building required huge quantities of timber – 20 hectares of mature oak woodland were required for constructing a navy gunship, much of it in special sizes and shapes (James 1981). Large tracts were planted in the Forest of Dean from 1668, and in the New Forest from 1698. The forests were selected for their close proximity to shipyards, because transport of wood was very difficult before the advent of the all-weather road. The Crown Forest policy was to plant oak only, because it was favoured for ships – a policy akin to today's simplistic emphases on 'miracle trees' or single-purpose planting schemes.

In the eighteenth and nineteenth centuries, however, naval timber needs were secured increasingly through imports from Maine and other colonies. This became a strong disincentive to plant at home. Yet, during the First World War, vast areas of private forest had to be felled for all sorts of purposes, and it became clear that timber imports were vulnerable to enemy bombardment. The Home-Grown Timber (Acland) Committee recommended that the run-down domestic forest reserves should once again be built up, but this time to provide for all purposes, especially in times of war and trade disruptions.

For this reason, the Forestry Commission was established in 1921, since when the area of productive forest in Great Britain has more than doubled. The Commission emphasized plantations on marginal land, with associated forestry research, training and careful site selection, so that afforestation would proceed according to 'scientific principles' (James 1981).

Tree plantations as aesthetic expressions and symbols of power

As planting became more widespread amongst the English leisured classes, there developed an increasingly sophisticated appreciation of the aesthetics of trees. Thomas notes that the ways in which landowners have managed their trees has reflected contemporary forms of social organization. As society liberalized in the eighteenth century, for example, tree cultivation became less regimented and there was reaction against 'mutilating' trees or carving them into 'unnatural shapes' through topiary, pollarding or shredding. The eighteenth century English landscape school planted trees in natural patterns, harmonizing with the surrounding landscape (Thomas 1983). And, with the increasing circulation of both aesthetic ideas and plant material across the world, landscape design was no longer limited to local traditions and species. (Jellicoe and Jellicoe, 1975).

The motives for planting amongst the gentry thus became:

a complex mixture of social assertiveness, aesthetic sense, patriotism and long-term profit. Together, they combined to make planting as much of an aristocratic obsession as dogs or horses. So it was that in England trees were not merely domesticated but gradually achieved an almost pet-like status.

(Thomas, 1983)

Planting for aesthetic purposes did not remain confined to the gentry. When, in the nineteenth century, Western Europe began transforming from a rural to an urban society, large-scale planting was employed for creating urban parks. By 1850, forestry had become a subject of general public interest (although 'forestry' was not yet a term in general use) (James 1981). Since this time, the urbanite has sought various forms of a rural aesthetic, perhaps in reaction to urban, industrialized life, and to the powerful forces of government and corporations that have shaped this life.

Natural woodlands and pastoral farmlands have been increasingly favoured by the public. Large-scale industrial forest plantations, particularly of clearly non-native species and for the benefit of state or corporations, have been disfavoured, echoing as they do the form and processes of mass production. Wordsworth abhorred the new plantations – the 'vegetable manufactories' – of the Lake District. It is suspected that public knowledge of the tax concessions obtained by rich people and corporations for planting has also contributed to plantations' low public esteem (Young 1991).

The greater part of the post-1945 planting in Britain was with exotic conifers, predominantly Sitka spruce *Picea sitchensis* on heathlands and rough pasture. In the 1970s and 1980s, there was much adverse criticism of the maturing – and therefore increasingly conspicuous – geometric monocultures by a public which was increasingly mobile, interested in natural history, and in search of countryside recreation. In response to these criticisms, the Forestry Commission introduced active landscape design, recreation management and wildlife conservation. None the less, the public perception remains that conifer plantations in rural areas are unattractive and poor for wildlife.

Currently, some of the biggest forestry plantation plans are for urban 'community forests', designed for the recreational needs of the ordinary town-dweller. It is intended that these will become mature forest that will be perceived as natural; they will be established using mixed broadleaves in swathes sympathetic to local landscapes. They may well be successful in this – for many people who otherwise find plantations execrable may be surprised to learn that the 'natural' forests which they hold in higher esteem are often the result of early plantations. Some ancient plantations in Europe, such as beechwoods in the Chilterns and oakwoods in the Troncais, are viewed as 'natural forests' by all except historians and botanists.

In summary, the enthusiasm for plantations in England evolved as a result of the Enclosure Acts; the increasing demand for wood – from the Royal and Merchant Navies, rapidly-developing industries and urban populations; and the associated commoditization of wood products. Widespread private planting took off only once the landowner was financially secure, was able to sell wood for the first time, and was confident of his tenure, so that his estate could be passed on to future generations of his family. State patronage ensured that plantations came to play integral parts in rural security, strategic timber supplies, industrial policy, fiscal policy and land-use patterns. Public reaction to state and corporate plantations – because they excluded important social and environmental benefits – has been counteracted increasingly effectively by these bodies in the last few decades.

The politics of plantations in industrial development: marginal land in France, Australia, South Africa

Perhaps the clearest illustration of large-scale planting leading to industrial development is provided by the Landes region of south-west France. Government planting began in the eighteenth century, to arrest the spread of sand dunes. It became very extensive, and community and private planting followed, for the native *Pinus pinaster* proved highly productive on the sandy soils. Resin, turpentine, pit props and railway sleepers supported a considerable rural industry in the nineteenth century, and pulp and paper mills followed in the twentieth. As Dargavel and Kengen (1992) note, the Landes plantations established the precedent that forest resources could be created on land too poor for agriculture, and hence without political controversy over its use.

The Landes model was to help with the great expansion of plantations, and rural industry, in Australia, New Zealand and South Africa in the 1930s. In Australia, the easily accessible forest supplies had been worked out soon after the rapid population expansion following the discovery of gold in 1851, and timber supplies had become limiting to industrial development. Funds from unemployment relief were contributed to afforestation, because there was also a strong notion that forestry provided healthy work for the unemployed during the depression. Plantations were established on wooded state land of low productivity, which was not contentious at the time. However, in the 1970s, this was criticized for degrading environmental values. Consequently, state planting took place on poor quality farmland; in the 1980s, this was criticized for its resultant social dislocation (Dargavel and Kengen 1992).

The politics of plantations in development: the modern period in the tropics

Tropical land in the service of European empires

In medieval Europe, land husbandry on its confined land base was characterized by intensive techniques. The European colonization of the 'New World', in contrast, afforded rich possibilities for expansion, and predatory forest use and agriculture came to characterize imperial European civilization. In some emergent settler cultures – perhaps most notably that of the USA – there evolved a mythology of boundless 'frontiers'. The profits from imperial agriculture and raw material shipment (including timber) helped to finance industries. The dynamic of industrial growth served in turn to sustain the mythology of unlimited frontiers, and further transformed these formative frontier myths into a belief in perpetual economic growth (Weiskel 1990).

The Europeans' main reason for tropical deforestation was cash crop production. West African cocoa was produced largely at the expense of forests. Burmese rice, for feeding the British Empire's labour force, was produced on cleared forest land. The Latin American coffee boom in the mid-nineteenth century was at the expense of hill forests; as was banana production in Central America at the turn of the century.

Certain natural forest products, notably timbers and spices, developed speciality markets, but accessible supplies were soon exhausted. The Portuguese logged dyewood on the north-east coast of Brazil (notably Brazilwood *Caesalpina*, after which the country was named). The Spanish cut Mahogany *Swietenia* on the Caribbean littoral of Central America; and many forests were completely removed by the early eighteenth century. The French opened up West African forests to harvest spices.

It was contrary to the early colonial frontier mentality to plant trees. Colonial forestry services took pride in being major contributors to the treasury, and were certainly not expected to make investments in long-term, unsure enterprises such as plantations. With few, short-lived exceptions, forestry services were not permitted to retain taxes for investment. On the contrary, there was an over-emphasis on revenue collection (Palmer 1989). In any case, there was rarely an economic incentive for planting: 'salvage' wood was obtainable from the agricultural clearance of forests and, at least initially, new forests were freely available when others were logged out. Thus, prior to the twentieth century, there were very few forest plantations in the tropics.

There were also local political reasons for colonial deforestation. Native forest dwellers derived considerable wealth and territorial security from natural forests. Wild forests were (and still are) considered to be havens for 'political dissidents', and hence serious threats to colonial rule. Colonial settlers cleared forests and enclosed the open land to secure territorial conquests. As a consequence, however, the settlers' agricultural (and later wood) production had to be concentrated close to settlements in easily-protected 'farm-like' plantations.

Once the colonies were under firm control, the plantation idea became widespread, especially for sugar, spice and rubber production. Systems of social control developed alongside plantations, the subdual of tropical nature being echoed by the subdual of its people. Indeed, as C.S. Lewis has observed, what we might simplistically perceive as man's domination of nature has more commonly been the domination of some men over other men, with nature as its instrument. The use of Amerindian and, later, African slave labour in West Indian sugar plantations is a clear example.

Large-scale colonial plantations of forest trees appeared much later than those for sugar, spices and rubber. They were mainly for military or other strategic needs, such as naval and construction timber, or for localized soil protection. They appeared after the period of slavery, but none the less alienated many people who had depended upon the land. The colonial authorities felt the need to simplify labour operations for, by and large, they could only work with local people if the latter were regimented in military fashion to undertake simple, repetitive actions. In some colonies, this tended to favour plantations over the more subtle arts of natural forest management, a tendency which later mechanization was also to encourage.

The oldest significant tropical timber plantations were of teak *Tectona grandis*, planted in the mid-nineteenth century, primarily for strategic reasons. (Teak had been tried on a small scale by the Dutch in Indonesia around 1650.) Shortly after 1800, the British Navy determined that teak forests along the Malabar coast could substitute for English oak in ship-building. Attempts to control teak extraction in Malabar District were unsuccessful, however, and in 1841 the East India Company ordered teak planting at Nilambur. The plantation's success was to ensure that, over the following century, one of the main purposes of British India's foresters was to establish teak plantations. Teak was subsequently planted throughout the tropics (Burma in 1856, Pakistan 1866, Bangladesh 1871, Java 1873, Vietnam 1908, Philippines 1910, Trinidad 1913) (Adlard 1992).

In the late nineteenth century, teak plantation objectives became more overtly commercial than strategic. Commercial plantation forestry, a long-term venture, was not viable until wild sources had been depleted; and was not possible until colonial administrations and relations with local people were both stable. Strong local markets were also important; usually, these developed towards the end of the colonial era, or at independence. Early commercial plantations for local markets in the tropics were of hardwoods, principally teak. Many of these were developed from earlier export-oriented plantations, as in Burma. MacGillivray (1990) has charted the changing policies and fortunes of Burmese teak plantations in detail [see Box 3.1].

Once large plantations were established, the relative success of different species became apparent, and the technical reasons for this were sought. From the nineteenth century, science was increasingly applied in the service of tropical forestry. Botanical explorations and botanic gardens helped to develop plantation possibilities, although their principal loyalty remained to agricultural development. Many promising species criss-crossed the continents. *Eucalyptus globulus* was introduced to India in 1843, to avert a fuelwood famine. Its success meant that *Eucalyptus* soon followed teak as a principal colonial tree; and hundreds of species and clones of *Eucalyptus* are now grown throughout the tropics and sub-tropics.

Environmental protection was frequently cited by colonial authorities as a reason for tree planting, although some commentators believe that this was sometimes a front for more exploitative intentions. An 1852 British Association report highlighted the environmental and social dangers of deforestation in India. Its environmental rationale contributed as much to the establishment of the Indian Forest Service as the requirement for teak, and led to extensive afforestation and forest protection in India (Grove 1990). (The colonial authorities were not, however, responsible for introducing the reforestation ethic to India. Earlier attempts at reforestation for environmental purposes had been made by the Amirs of Sind between 1785 and 1840.)

Plantations were established in late colonial Kenya, Tanganyika (Tanzania) and Northern Rhodesia (Zambia) from 1950 to 1960, partly to take the pressure off natural forests. These plantations, largely cypress and pine, have indeed reduced the industrial pressure on natural woodlands, but subsistence pressures remain high. Extensive softwood plantations were also established in Kenya following the Mau-Mau revolt, during which the authorities had strategically deforested land to deprive the Mau-Mau of sanctuary (Spears 1991).

However, colonial plantations were more frequently made by the removal of natural forests, which, at the time, were considered 'inferior' and politically uncontentious. Trinidadian *Mora* forests made way for teak, and forests in Madagascar were removed for *Eucalyptus*. The scientific arguments in favour of plantations were narrow and could not always be substantiated, in part because there had been no experience of complete rotations.

Twentieth century industrial plantations in the tropics: independent states and the private sector

The large-scale industrial forest plantation in the tropics is a phenomenon of the last four decades. Newly-independent governments and corporations have made substantial investments, initially in hardwoods, but increasingly in softwoods.

The spread of industrial softwood plantations can be correlated with the change from agrarian, mercantilist societies to more industrial, capital-intensive societies. Softwood plantations can employ economies of scale in producing large quantities of uniform, cheap, fast-growing material suitable for industry.

By the 1950s, it was well established that light-demanding softwoods grew better in plantation than the shade-tolerant/demanding hardwoods favoured by commerce. Biological constraints had hindered the earliest softwood developments, however. For example, although tropical pines had been experimented with in the nineteenth century, industrial plantations could not take off until the importance of mycorrhizal root associations had been established.

Once fundamental technical issues were resolved, softwood plantations were established by the majority of governments in the latter half of the twentieth century. These were mainly for exporting raw materials and for building up a domestic industrial raw materials base; but also partly for supplying rural subsistence needs and tackling environmental problems.

In the 1950s and 1960s, it was widely believed that development would 'trickle down' from industrial growth. The case that investment in industrial forestry could stimulate industry in developing countries was made by Westoby (1962). This approach was strongly adhered to by the FAO and development agencies, and led to much investment in industrial plantations, at least until the 1970s. Development planning and aid more easily accommodated investment in plantations, as opposed to natural forest management, which is riddled with uncertainties.

Ironically, although plantations are more intimately linked to the (global) industrial sector than any other forestry activity, governments have been notoriously poor at examining these links and their economic consequences. Many plantations were established with inadequate cost-benefit analysis or social and environmental impact assessment. This is perhaps because efficiency appraisal was a relatively new requirement in government operations; and because the development of plantations has taken place over many years, during which objectives have changed (industrial development, employment, conservation, strategic supplies, decentralization, balance of payments, etc.) (Dargavel and Kengen 1992). Consequently, there are many 'white elephants'. For example, plantations in Malawi were designed to supply a major pulp mill, but were subsequently found to be uneconomic for pulp.

The failure of many expensive, government-run plantations in the tropics has hence been ascribed to poorly-formulated and unstable forest policy and operational and financial capabilities, but also to many basic, even banal, management problems. In Gabon, Liberia and Cameroon, government plantation failures have been attributed to cuts in forestry department budgets (Rietbergen 1989). In recent decades, it has become clear that some corporations can provide – far more sustainably than can governments – the stability and resources required for tropical plantation investment (Schmidheiny 1992).

In the nineteenth century, private involvement in forestry meant deforestation. Private planting was, with few exceptions, for rubber and oil, tea and coffee and tropical fruit, rather than for timber. Private timber concerns played little part in afforestation during the colonial era, and concentrated on the trade of natural forest timber. Private interest in plantations picked up only when forestry could be mechanized, and as forest product prices rose. For these reasons, afforestation greatly increased in the latter half of the twentieth century ; and almost all of the major plantations were established after 1950, many by corporations (Kanowski and Savill 1990). Plantations were found to be more amenable to corporate techniques than natural forests, and their boundaries easier to protect.

It was the depletion of North American pulpwood forests (which before 1960 dominated the pulp industry), and the realization that tropical and subtropical plantations could produce pulpwood faster and cheaper, that precipitated a major movement of pulp company capital to southern climates (Marchak 1992). Perhaps the first plantations designed solely for pulp were those of the Usutu Pulp Company in Swaziland. Begun in 1948, by 1957 they had become the largest plantation in Africa. Predominantly under *Pinus patula*, today the 52,000 hectares produce solely Kraft wood pulp, which forms Swaziland's second most important export (Adlard 1992). Corporations have become increasingly adept at identifying and seizing plantation opportunities in the tropics, especially since the mid-1970s' oil price rises, when the potential of wood biofuels led to a boom in plantation investment.

Corporations have been able to draw on the early plantation management experience. As Kanowski and Savill (1990) note, general management techniques for teak in India (e.g. Griffith 1942), and for subtropical pines in southern Africa (e.g. Craib 1947), were largely established prior to corporate involvement. Suitable species, or at least genera, for various sites throughout the British Commonwealth were known (e.g. Streets 1962), even if management regimes and different genetic material had not been tested.

Earlier plantations were established with limited access to genetic material, and it soon became apparent that poor material was a major constraint to performance. State and corporate tree selection and breeding programmes have shown good genetic gain – principally in poplars, pines and eucalypts. In Brazil, as early as 1910, the Paulista Railway Company began testing and planting *Eucalyptus*, eventually trying 144 species (Dargavel and Kengen 1992).

Pines have become the most commonly planted conifer. Afforestation in South Africa of *Pinus patula* during the 1920s was very successful; it led to the dominance of that species in other southern African countries. Very large, commercially-viable, export-oriented plantations have been built up since 1950 in Chile, South Africa and New Zealand, concentrating on *Pinus radiata*.

The introduction of new species for commercial plantations has sometimes led to spectacular failures – which may partly explain commercial conservativeness in species choice. *Gmelina arborea* was introduced for Daniel Ludwig's enormous Jari pulpwood production scheme in Brazil, which began in 1968. His team did not realize that only 25 per cent of the area was suitable for the species; and that local leaf cutter ants were serious pests of *Gmelina*. Had Ludwig examined the historical experience of *Gmelina* in Burma – recorded as early as 1910 – he could have avoided some very expensive mistakes.

The choice of *Gmelina* was not Ludwig's only mistake, however. Heavy equipment and high technology harvesting proved unsuitable, as it compacted and eroded the soil. Civil engineers, and not foresters, managed the plantations. Work-crew contractors were notorious for their treatment of workers brought in from the poor north-eastern states. Labour turnover was as high as 200–300 per cent a year, and there were 30 directors over the fourteen-year life of the project. Finally, as Brazil moved closer to democracy, Ludwig could no longer count on the support of military presidents. The social and economic unsustainability of the plantation became all too apparent, and Ludwig sold it in 1982 to a Brazilian consortium (Denslow and Padoch 1988).

By 1982, however, many of the basic lessons had been learned in Jari. Under Brazilian ownership, with rapid-feedback silvicultural research programmes, and more suitable species such as *Pinus caribaea var. hondurensis* and *Eucalyptus deglupta*, Jari has become one of the most successful commercial plantations in the tropics, underpinned by the huge demand for paper.

Because technical lessons have been learned, industrial afforestation in the tropics has been able to mushroom. However, this rapid afforestation has been without good social and environmental precedents, and many schemes have had high social and environmental costs.

> In a broad sense . . . plantation forestry has been less sussessful than was hoped . . . The failure of plantation forests to satisfy many of the demands made on forest resources can be attributed to a variety of factors peculiar to each case. Technical limitations have contributed on occasions; however, in general, the more fundamental causes have been failure to appreciate and accommodate the political economy of land and forest use, and the definition of management objectives which concentrated excessively on the production of wood for industrial use.
>
> (Kanowski and Savill 1990)

Peoples' plantations in the twentieth century tropics: 'agroforestry' and 'participatory' forestry

'Agroforestry' describes land-use systems and technologies where trees and other woody perennials are used on the same land as agricultural crops or animals (Lundgren and Raintree 1982). Many believe that agroforestry is a novel concept. In fact, it is the separation of agriculture from forestry which is more recent.

The custom in Europe, at least until land enclosure, was to clear-fell forest, burn the slash, cultivate food crops for varying periods and then plant or sow trees among agricultural crops. Such agroforestry systems were still widely practised in Finland until the late nineteenth century, and in parts of Germany until 1920. The principal objective of early European systems was not forestry production, but food production. By the end of the nineteenth century, however, the forest crop had taken over as the principal agroforestry objective. This reflected a change in political power away from the peasant – whose principal need was food cultivation – towards the state – which needed timber, but which nevertheless recognized that timber production could be compromised unless local needs were accommodated (King 1989).

Traditional agroforestry is still practised all over the tropics. As in Europe, such systems evolved principally to grow food. In contrast, the establishment of forest crops was the main reason for the colonial authorities' evolution of 'taungya' systems in the tropics.

In 1806, a Karen in Burma established teak through a system he called taungya (taung – hill, ya – cultivation). Farmers were contracted to plant teak, but were also permitted to use the land between the tree seedlings in early years to raise crops. Sir Dietrich Brandis of the Indian Forest Service was impressed, and the system spread through Burma, to Chittagong, Bengal and then further to South Africa and Trinidad. Today, the system is practised throughout the tropics, with other species as well as teak. Taungya became widespread once it was known that plantations were more productive than natural forests, and so there was an imperative to replace natural forests. It was also known that plantation establishment was costly; and that plantations were vulnerable to the predations of peasants. So 'the ruling philosophy was to establish forest plantations whenever possible through the utilization of available unemployed or landless labourers' (King 1989).

Taungya almost always reflects a political compromise – of local needs for food with state needs for timber. Early taungya was almost entirely an instrument for obtaining state needs, being designed for meeting afforestation targets efficiently. All research was aimed at ensuring that the forest crop – and not the agricultural crop – fared best in the association. The farmer was often exploited; taungya relied on land hunger and unemployment; and demanded the removal of the farmer after some years.

After 1970, however, more thought was given to the farmer and the agricultural aspects of the system, because it was evident that failure to do so had compromised even the forestry objectives. Furthermore, in the 1970s, there was a much greater concern for increasing food supplies and rural incomes, and for protecting the environment. Re-examination of the policies of the FAO, the World Bank and other assistance agencies – which hitherto had supported 'Green Revolution' agricultural packages beyond the means of poorer rural farmers – resulted in a surge of support to agroforestry. By this time, the 'trickle-down' theory of development arising from industrialization had been discredited. Frank (1969, quoted in Dargavel and Kengen 1992), after studying Brazil and Chile, claimed that the benefits of industrial development trickled not down, but up, to the dominant countries of the world economic order. And, by 1978, Westoby had to agree that the 'famous multiplier effects [of forestry] are missing' (Westoby 1978).

Modern agroforestry began in the 1970s, based on the premises that: crop-livestock-tree associations could contribute significantly to both agriculture and forestry; that there were ways of optimizing the yields of both agricultural and forest crops; and that agroforestry could be a viable land management system in its own right. Agroforestry has since become a quite distinct discipline. It is one from which plantation foresters – in their need to integrate plantations into increasingly complex land use mosaics – can learn much.

'**Social forestry**' appeared on the scene following 1970, for reasons similar to those behind modern agroforestry. Initially, it was largely a product of development aid, spurred on by the donors' perceived need to grow more fuelwood, and by humanitarian concerns following natural disasters, such as the Sahelian droughts (Arnold 1991). Early social forestry thus had a high tendency towards quick and dramatic 'fixes', and was heavily dependent upon single techniques and species. For example, it accelerated the trend at the time to search for 'miracle trees'. There was excessive emphasis on industrial species such as *Eucalyptus* which proved unsuitable for meeting local multiple needs (Kanowski and Savill 1990). Social forestry failed to take an adequately integrated view of the diversity of ecological, economic, legal and social factors. Whereas it was thought that peasants would undertake 'community forestry' projects purely for subsistence, it is now recognized that financial factors provide major incentives for planting – even for people supposedly outside the market system (Arnold 1991). Newer forms of 'participatory forestry' base themselves on local definitions of needs and approaches, and local monitoring of results.

Today, the trend to 'socialize' all forestry continues. There is concern about the failure of governments and corporations to deliver forest goods and services to the poor on (increasingly) nationalized, or corporation-controlled, land:

> Because nearly all the forest and forest industry development which has taken place in the underdeveloped world over the last decades has been externally oriented . . . the basic forest products needs of the peoples of the underdeveloped world are further from being satisfied than ever. . . . The role which forestry could play in supporting agriculture and raising rural welfare has been either badly neglected or completely ignored.
>
> (Westoby 1975)

There are movements to return to local systems of control over resources, such as existed before colonial times. The well-known Chipko crusade which developed in India in the early 1970s is, in fact, a revival of a seventeenth-century women's movement for 'tree hugging' in Rajasthan. The modern Indian experience continues to reveal many interesting lessons in regaining community/local control of forests (see e.g. Poffenberger 1990). India is not unique, however. The rise of democracy in South America in the 1980s has led to a significant return of control of forests and resources to local people; it has also allowed a more open challenging of large industrial projects – including plantations – that had hitherto been imposed on local people and their environments (Dean 1992).

Conclusions

The lessons of history

Forests and wood have been major determinants of history. Wood has been a basic material for development in all its 'stages' and *per caput* wood requirements have tended to increase as nations have developed.

For many centuries in many countries, there have been traditions of **small-scale** plantations for specialized material, aesthetic, cultural and religious purposes. These small plantations have usually been maintained within intricate mosaics of land use. Their techniques have largely been ignored in industrial plantation development.

In contrast, **industrial** plantations have had only a short and discontinuous history of supplying wood, confined largely to the twentieth century, and in response to urgent political and economic imperatives for building up forest resources.

Industrial forestry plantations have been encouraged by:

- overexploitation of natural forests; where remaining forests become economically inaccessible;
- people being excluded from natural forests, notably by land enclosure, and requiring alternative wood supplies;
- the availability of (marginal) land for which there are no politically-contentious competing uses;
- secure tenure of land available for planting;
- strategic imperatives to build up wood supplies, notably after war;
- strong and growing markets for uniform wood products, in large quantities for industrial uses;
- adequate investment finance at low opportunity cost;
- stability in all the policies and authorities that affect forestry and investment;
- official incentives and promotion of planting;
- biases inherent in development planning, aid and finance (plantations being easier to plan and operate than the more uncertain natural forest management);
- religious and aesthetic canons and expression;
- the example of visionary, forward-looking leaders in society;
- the need to protect environmentally-fragile land and to reclaim land in a cost-effective manner.

Industrial forestry plantations have been discouraged by:

- absence of the above incentives;
- the availability of cheap wood imports;
- the high price of capital in many rapidly-developing economies;
- policy and economic signals which favour short-term agricultural production over plantation forestry on cleared land;
- technology changes, e.g. from fuelwood-using to electricity-using;
- erroneous forecasting of demands for forest products, e.g. the 1930s lack

of investment in plantations because forecasters believed that concrete and steel would replace wood.

Industrial development and growing populations have sometimes conflicted in their demands for wood resources, with varying results. Plantations have been established by both industry and social groups, but the demands of industry have often been dominant.

Many industrial plantations have been imposed on local people. Plantations have taken land out of food production; alienated people from their land; and devastated culturally important species, habitats and landscapes. The failure to deal with social realities has been responsible for many examples of poor plantation performance in this century. New methods, skills and training are still needed to help plantation foresters deal better with social and cultural issues. The high visibility of the mistakes of the earliest plantation developments in the twentieth century has meant that much of the public retains a poor impression of plantations.

Plantations established for narrow purposes have often failed, especially in an unstable economic and sociopolitical climate, and where they serve external ends irrespective of local needs and desires. If plantations which initially were narrowly-focused have eventually succeeded, this has frequently been because they adapted to provide for more purposes. For example, recreational and environmental purposes have been added to 'commercial' plantations; and financial objectives have been added to ostensibly 'social' forestry projects.

Multipurpose plantations that include environmental and social objectives from the beginning would appear to be more adaptable and sustainable than 'pure' environmental or social forestry. Yet there are few historical examples, aside from small-scale traditional schemes, from which to gain insight.

In future, plantations are likely to form an increasing proportion of forests:

- The predicted gap between wood demand and supply in many regions is so large that only plantations can fill it quickly enough.
- It is difficult to protect natural forests from excessive exploitation, but in contrast easier to protect the boundaries and control the use of plantations. Investment will hence be preferentially attracted to plantations.
- There are global economic and social trends which will encourage policy-makers and the market to value forest goods and services more

highly, to manage forests more carefully, to take products from forests of low biodiversity value, and to increase the area of forests. All of these may encourage plantations.

The need for further historical research:

Finally, a note on some of the gaps in our knowledge of plantation history, and suggestions for research:

The phenomenon of industrial plantations in the tropics is recent, and has not been subject to adequate historical study; moreover, it has occurred in a period of considerable social and economic flux – that of 'Third World development' – which itself has yet to be authoritatively traced and interpreted. In contrast, the body of historical analysis of English forestry is more robust, and is enriched by much social and economic history. (This is why this chapter has discussed England in some depth; and why our conclusions on the lessons of history can only be preliminary for the tropics.)

The growing body of historical literature on tropical deforestation could usefully be supplemented by case studies of the converse phenomenon, tropical afforestation. Historical work on the global, post-1950 mushrooming of tropical plantations, in the context of the powerful state and corporate forces behind them, could provide valuable insights for the increased afforestation efforts that are almost universally proposed for the future. Of special practical value would be the preparation of national forest histories, examining the linkages between natural forests and plantations.

To do this work, we suggest a partnership of local foresters (who, on the whole, have been good at keeping records) with local historians (who are trained to analyse records in their social, cultural and economic contexts). For national and local forest histories, we would add other professions in the humanities, and especially local groups; these would describe historical changes in local forests and expose the value of these changes as expressed by local people. Contemporary forest policy research would be considerably strengthened by explanations of evolving local forest values, and of the historical background to forest policies and administrations.

BOX 3.1
Poplars and willows: the emergence of important plantation trees

The *Salicaceae* (poplars and willows) were amongst the first trees to be

---

domesticated. When the forests and plains of western Asia and the eastern Mediterranean were cleared for agriculture, river banks and gravelly alluvial plains which were poor in humus were left aside, because no worthwhile crops could be expected from them. On such soils in the Euphrates, the Po and the Danube, poplars and willows flourished, and people came to look to these trees for satisfying timber and fuelwood needs.

Poplar and willow were cut regularly. It was found that they sprouted well after cutting, and the cuttings provided an effective means of propagation. Management regimes developed to favour the production of specific products, e.g. coppicing for firewood and poles, pollarding where livestock were present, and regular pruning to increase yields of forage and litter. All these regimes produced wooded areas that became prominent features in the Eurasian landscape.

Poplar and willow cuttings can withstand fairly rough treatment: they were transported successfully from Afghanistan over high Karakorum and Pamir passes even in the depths of winter, to be planted in irrigated mountain desert oases. Gradually, as each community began to understand the management and performance of the species, vegetative material was improved to meet local needs. In the high plateaus of Kashmir, as well as Turkey, Iran, Iraq, Syria and Afghanistan, poplar and willow remain of extreme importance to the subsistence economy, but the selection of planting material has been rudimentary. In contrast, where there was a strong financial motive, selection and breeding has progressed.

In the seventeenth century, North American poplar species (notably *Populus deltoides*) began to be introduced into Europe. Natural and, later, bred hybrids (with *P. nigra*) appeared, and these grew particularly well. The Marquis di Cavour imported some 'Canadian' poplars and planted them near Turin. Their rapid growth and ease of propagation led to high demand, and the first poplar nurseries were established to meet it. It was quickly appreciated that, even though these trees were from the same source in Canada, they could be differentiated into varieties with common attributes – which were matched with clients' needs rather than according to taxonomic differences.

Around 1900, Italian paper manufacturers developed a way of making mechanical pulp from poplar, and several promotional drives were made to get farmers to plant poplar crops of selected varieties. When sanctions were imposed on Italy during the Abyssinian War, Italian plywood manufacturers had to give up tropical timbers and turn to home-grown poplar. The area of farm poplar plantations increased dramatically. From the 1930s, a private paper firm, the Cartiere Burgo Society, developed research programmes and an extension service, which encouraged further private planting on farms. It has since worked on more than a million hybrids and established clones for use throughout the world.

Today, Italy continues to lead the poplar industry, and – throughout Europe – poplar has remained largely an agricultural crop. Its fast growth rate and very high fertilization needs have meant that, unlike other plantation species which have to be grown on politically uncontentious marginal land, poplar can compete financially with agriculture. Poplar can even be grown as part of a rotation (although generally annual crops and poplars are grown separately on the most appropriate land on the farm). Poplar is just as important, however, in social forestry schemes, partricularly in Western Asia, where its fast growth and multi-purpose capabilities are important.

S.B.

Principal source: FAO, *Poplars and willows in wood production and land use*, Rome: FAO, 1980.

BOX 3.2

Forest plantations in Japan's development

'Eight out of ten mountains in the nation are deforested': thus lamented a Confucian scholar in early seventeeth century Japan.

The pressures on Japan's forests had indeed become unsustainable by the seventeenth century. The needs of Japan's burgeoning peasantry for charcoal, lumber and green manure, and the extensive city and castle reconstruction that took place following the wars of the previous century, had depleted the forests. Large-sized timber, especially of favoured species such as cypress, oak and cedar, became in short supply.

One by one, the 300 fief administrations, influenced by Confucian ecological philosophies, introduced forest control measures. These curtailed harvesting and licensed the peasantry's consumption of wood. However, these measures were inadequately enforced, and in any case were inappropriate in light of Japan's increasing forest product needs. The requirement for plantations became clear.

In 1671, Lord Tsugaru Nobumasa planted one million saplings of cedar and pine, and many fiefs followed his example. A century later, tree planting had become routine and systematic, with a rotation of cutting sites and compulsory reforestation. Some lords instituted further conditions: peasants had to tend the planted trees; the logged forest had to be improved, such as by planting cedar whenever pine was felled; and licences to fell trees were issued only when seedlings were first planted (the obligatory ratio of saplings to felled trees ranging from two to a hundred). In certain districts, however, it was difficult to enforce these regulations, and large backlogs of unplanted saplings were built up.

Nevertheless, by the time imperial rule was restored in 1868, a tradition of forest conservation and afforestation had been instituted in Japan. This was to provide a good basis with which to ensure good supplies of timber, fuelwood, silk and water for the developing urban areas and industry – indeed, to assist Japan's economic 'take off'. By 1900, two-thirds of Japan's woodlands had been transferred from the ownership of the lords to the Imperial Household or government; this secured government revenue to pay for infrastructure development. It also ensured that afforestation was easier to organize and forest exploitation was more effectively regulated. The fact that Japan's increases in food production came from intensification, rather than extension into the forest, was undoubtedly also important for the sustainability of its forest industry.

Yet this development was bought at a price. Peasants' traditional rights to use forest land and trees were frequently eliminated, leaving them acutely short of timber, fuel and fodder. This led to arson, and the neglect of afforestation at local level. Resistance was suppressed through military or police force. However, in some areas where locals most fiercely opposed forest nationalization, 'profit-sharing forests' were established; the state owned the forest, but locals contributed to afforestation and management, and received a share of the harvest.

In 1899, the state forest management programme began, and was to run for sixteen years. It surveyed all of Japan's forests, sold suboptimal ones, prepared management plans for the remainder and – by far the most ambitious – planted 550,000 hectares of model plantations.

Hence, in order to respond to increasingly complex demands for forest products, Japanese forestry had moved strongly in favour of plantations; complemented by the natural forests of best potential, which had been identified and reserved through a well-organized process. It had also been recognized that the assurance of secure tenure was essential for sustaining both plantations and natural forests.

After the Second World War, when the forests had been heavily exploited for military purposes (even the roots of pine trees were exploited for aircraft fuel), an even larger plantation programme was launched. This included well-designed incentives to encourage private plantations, and three million hectares were reforested in less than twenty years.

At present, however, most domestic plantations cannot compete with imported tropical wood. This is because of: the very high cost of labour in Japan, and hence neglect of labour-intensive operations such as thinning; undeveloped access infrastructure, where many plantations are on steep slopes; mounting pressure from alternative land uses, together with the constraints of a fragmented forest ownership structure; and – most topical at present – the ability of the Japanese to capture excessive rents from tropical forests.

S.B.

Principal sources:
Bazett, M., *Industrial Wood*, Shell Tree Plantation Review Series, Study No.3, London: Shell International, 1992.
Kotari, K., *Initial Hardships of the Japanese State Forest in late 19th Century*, voluntary paper for ITTO Conference of Senior Foresters, Yokohama, 1991.
Osako, M.M., 'Forest preservation in Tokugawa Japan' in Tucker R.P. and Richards, J.F. (Eds), *Global deforestation and the nineteenth century world economy*, 1983.

BOX 3.3

Teak plantations in Burma: a story of policy inconsistency

Large teak plantations were established by the British in Burma from the 1850s. The extraction of teak *Tectona grandis* from Burma's natural forests had been perhaps the most intensive in nineteenth-century colonial forestry, and a severe shortage of teak was expected.

From 1860 to 1939, teak plantations were established for export. The area planted annually was highly erratic; this was because plantation policy altered course frequently, according to:

- changing assessments of the economic viability of teak over its 100-year-plus rotation;
- difficulties in assessing future teak markets;
- changing assessments of the silvicultural possibilities of producing high-quality timber;
- the Forest Department's failure to work well with local people, experiencing difficulties in obtaining 'willing labour' from the 'wild tribes' through the taungya method;
- theft from plantations; and
- the fluctuating budget of the Forest Department, which fell greatly in the Depression.

By 1920, the good growth of the Burmese teak plantations, and their suitability for the colonial authorities' regimented management style, meant that plantations were in great favour. By this time, however, it was becoming clear that several environmental hazards could render plantations inviable over their long rotation: the repeated occurrence of fire in plantations; the high incidence of bee-hole borer; attacks from various defoliators; and soil erosion.

A few years later, the Depression meant that teak export markets all but disappeared. Only local markets could be found. Forest Department pessimism was compounded, however, for it became widely believed that iron, steel and concrete would eventually subsitute for hardwoods such as teak. In 1935, the Government of Burma ruled 'that in view of the speculative nature of the investment and the long rotation necessary to obtain timber of the quality required, further planting of teak for export should cease'. Planting for the internal market was deemed acceptable, but only the most promising of 43,000 ha of existing plantations were to continue to receive public funds. In practice, planting was carried out for village supply only, and not even for national industrial markets.

In 1980, however, the independent Government of Burma again launched a major teak planting programme for export, but at a much larger scale, up to 38,000 ha per year in mixtures with other species. There are many possible reasons for the renewed interest in teak plantations in Burma: the difficulties of natural forest management; the low opportunity cost of land and labour; the need to generate foreign exchange; and more recently the logging ban in Thailand and the possibilities of remunerative markets for tropical hardwoods from proven 'sustainable' sources such as plantations. The signs are, however, that Burma's national teak forests have been overexploited in recent years.

S.B.

Principal source: MacGillivray, A.W., *Forest use and conflict in Burma 1750–1990*, Thesis, University of London, 1990.

CHAPTER 4

HOW MUCH WOOD DO WE NEED?

Alf Leslie

The production of wood is the main reason for today's industrial forest plantation programmes. This does not mean that wood production is necessarily the most important purpose of plantations. It does mean, however, that the future need for wood and wood products is a realistic starting point for any review of plantations. Wood production has put tight limits on such technical plantation matters as the choice of species, sites and mangement regimes and, to a lesser degree, on forestry institutional arrangements.

It is, therefore, important to have a reasonably reliable idea of how much wood will be needed in future. At first sight there does not seem to be any overwhelming difficulty about this. All that might be involved is to work out how much wood an individual needs to maintain an adequate quality of life, and to multiply that by the population of the area concerned. This is, essentially, the procedure underlying the wood forecasts of earlier times. However, almost without exception, such forecasts incorrectly pointed to imminent local, national or even global timber famines. The fact that none of the predicted famines has occurred suggests that the simple, obvious procedure does not reliably estimate how much wood will be needed.

Forecasting wood demands

After the Second World War, the consumption of timber increased on an unprecedentedly rapid scale. The first wave came with large-scale economic and social reconstruction, mainly in the developed countries. This accelerated with the demand for industrial wood in the rapidly-recovering, indeed expanding, economies. In turn, this triggered two concurrent developments. The first was approaches to deal with the possibility of recurring timber shortages; the second a sustained effort to improve and refine timber demand forecasting. All of this has run parallel to, and may in fact have been derived from, the increasingly sophisticated econometric work in economic and development planning. So much so that, at times, the current interest in forecasting timber demand lies more in the technique than the results. Certainly, whatever the cause, much less emphasis is now given to long-term studies of timber trends than was the case twenty years ago.

At least two factors account for the shift in emphasis to techniques rather than forecasts. The first is that the more sophisticated and realistic forecasts were no more reliable (with one notable exception) than the earlier, simpler methods. The exception was pulp and paper, in which forecasts based on firm relationships with clearly-identified demand shifters were spectacularly accurate for the two decades up to 1975. The second is that attention at world level was directed away from industrial wood to the fuelwood and subsistence timber needs of the least-developed countries. And perhaps a third factor was the declining faith in economic planning.

An interesting by-product was the secondary literature which developed in what might be termed the philosophy of timber demand forecasting. Distinctions were clarified between projections and forecasts. Terms such as 'prospects', 'outlooks' and 'forward estimates' were introduced to avoid the prophetic implications of forecasting. Attempts were made to have the economic distinctions between the terms 'needs', 'requirements', 'demand' and 'consumption' recognized and universally adopted.

The effects of all these advances have been rather mixed. On the one hand, there is no doubt that analysts have become much more precise in stating what they are producing. The recent studies by FAO are, for instance, described quite unambiguously as 'projections' (FAO 1986 and 1988) or 'forecasts based on projections' (ECE/FAO 1986). These distinctions were not always apparent in FAO's earlier work. The users of such work, on the other hand, are nothing like as cautious or as discriminating. On the whole they tend to take the projections, outlooks, perspectives, or whatever they are called, as authoritative forecasts almost unconditionally, with little regard for whatever qualifications may be attached.

For the analysts, Clarke (1979) offers the basic text:

The prophecies and predictions of the last 200 years show that the future is not accurately predictable on any scale in any detail. There are too many variables and no-one can guess what changes may direct the apparent direction of human development.

So why do they do it? Clarke again has the answer:

. . . for they offer the only means by which individuals and nations can find their direction in a changing world.

To assess, then, how much wood we are going to need we have two possibilities. The first is to select a level which looks appropriate from amongst the existing projections or forecasts. The catch, however, is that while there are plenty to choose from, these is little guidance as to how to choose. The second is to work it out for ourselves. This may, in fact, be the more practical way to proceed in many circumstances.

Needs for wood

In doing so, we have first to examine the implications of another difficulty, the meaning of 'needs'. Thanks to the FAO yearbooks of Forest Products we have a good idea of how much wood the world now uses, by wood product category and by country. Since the series now covers forty years, it is possible to trace the evolution of production, trade and consumption of wood as a whole or by categories in any combination of countries. It is, for forestry, one of the most valuable sets of statistics produced by any organization. Overall, therefore, it is a superb basis for trend studies and for making projections or forecasts from trends.

Nevertheless, neither production nor consumption has any equivalence with needs. The amount consumed at any given time is a function of the interaction of demand and supply through the price mechanism. This means that consumption can vary with changing prices. Hence to regard consumption as measuring needs leads to need being dependent on price, which is something of a contradiction.

The point is that economics deals with wants, not needs, and then only registers those wants which are backed by the necessary purchasing or political power to make them effective. Consumption, and the statistics relating to it, cannot therefore measure needs. Yet, as everyone knows, there are many people who are in dire need of the basic essentials for a reasonable standard of living, but lack the means to acquire them. The weakness in consumption-based, or more generally, market-based analysis is not, therefore, so much the economic error of equating consumption with requirements. Rather it is more fundamental; it simply cannot project or forecast the need for wood.

Market-based analysis has a further weakness: a great deal of what is registered as consumption cannot, by any stretch of imagination, be regarded as filling any real need. Veblen's analysis of conspicuous consumption (1957) and Galbraith's concept of market creation (1958) make this point at the level of the economy generally, while Westoby (1974) made a stinging criticism of the unnecessary consumption generated by the paper industry. The once- or twice-only use of plywood for concrete form-work is another example of consumption overstating need; and almost any building site will show that an appreciable amount of the recorded consumption of sawn wood is not actually used.

Two plausible, but fallacious, conclusions can be drawn from this. The first is that it is pointless to assess the need for wood, because there is little prospect of basic needs being supplied to those who cannot afford more than bare survival. Harsh as the conclusion is, it could be argued that any realistic assessment of the future need for wood has to be market-based, and must ignore what the need in a perfect world might be.

The second conclusion is to assume that those figures for recorded consumption which **understate** needs (e.g. wood for housing the poor) simply cancel out the figures which **overstate** needs (e.g. wood used and wasted in housing and servicing the wealthy).

Both conclusions are erroneous. No amount of casuistry can make effective demand the measure of need; and the assumption that wasteful consumption and unmet need are equal quantities in calculating total consumption can only be a guess. Nevertheless, this does provide a convenient base from which to make a first approximation of the amount of wood needed. On this understanding, we can get an idea of the magnitude of the issue from some of the recent projections.

Projections for the next thirty years

The world uses, annually, around 3.7 billion m^3 of wood in roundwood measure. Slightly more than half is used for fuel, and slightly under half for industrial purposes, mainly in construction and paper manufacture. This annual demand on the world's forests thus amounts to approximately $1m^3$ per hectare, which hardly puts them under great strain. On the contrary, it could be taken as evidence that the world's forests are not being utilized efficiently. Even allowing for the fact that consumption (or removals, which is the more correct term) understates the volume actually felled, the annual forest depletion deriving from wood demand is well below the rate of growth. In other words, at the **global** level, the present rate of wood use is potentially sustainable.

Table 4.1 Projections of world consumption of industrial roundwood to the year 2040

	Million M^3 rounded to nearest 10 million						
Source or base				*Year*			
	Mean 1987–8	1990	2000	2010	2020	2030	2040
Recorded 1.	1,660						
FAO 1986		1,410	1,810				
FAO 1988		1,660	2,080				
1987–8 Projected at constant annual rate of increase of:							
1.0%		1,700	1,900	2,090	2,300	2,530	2,950
1.5%		1,740	2,020	2,340	2,700	3,140	3,640
2.0%		1,770	2,160	2,630	3,170	3,870	4,720

Note 1: FAO *Yearbook of Forest Products* 1988 (production data)

The increase in industrial wood consumption of 400–420 million m^3 projected over the next ten years by FAO (1986 and 1988) hardly makes any difference (Table 4.1). Nor for that matter would the 500 million m^3 increase in fuelwood consumption projected at the rate of growth experienced over the last decade. The drain on forests would still represent less than half the wood added by growth, even after deducting deforested areas. However, ten years is not at all long enough to gauge the dynamics of wood supply.

Therefore we are forced into making our own forecasts. The official forecasts do not extend global coverage beyond the year 2000. Some of the regional ones do go further, e.g. the fourth ECE/FAO European Timber Trends Study (1986) goes up to 2025, although in rather less detail, and the Basic Plan for Japan (Government of Japan 1980) looks ahead to 2026. One way of making a longer-term forecast for ourselves is to project at a selected rate of growth, constant or changing, along the lines of the FAO (1986) study. The results of such an exercise are summarized in Table 4.1. For reasons to be discussed later, this approach is a stopgap at best. But at this stage, no more is needed than an idea of the order of changing needs for wood over the relatively long period it takes in forestry to increase the sustainable wood supply. Thirty years hence, as Table 4.1 shows, the consumption of wood may have approximately doubled, projecting at the rate of increase experienced in the recent past.

This gives an entirely different outlook from that given by the prospects for the next ten years alone. Over thirty years, the surviving natural forest will be hard-pressed to maintain adequate supplies of industrial wood, let alone to meet the fuelwod demand (Leslie 1991). If substantial additional areas are withdrawn from wood production to satisfy agricultural and environmental interests, and operational restrictions are imposed on the remainder, then the world's forests could move in twenty years from meeting the needs for wood easily to becoming heavily over-cut. The case for plantations is then clear.

Plantations could easily replace natural forests as the source of most of the world's wood: the 1990 world consumption of wood is equivalent to the annual increment of about 300 million hectares of plantations. With some elementary intensification over current plantation techniques, a global plantation resource of 250 million hectares would be plenty. Even if the consumption of wood continued to increase at the 1.5 per cent per annum experienced over the last twenty years, an addition of around 3 million hectares a year would be enough to sustain the rising demand.

With a present world plantation resource around 135 million hectares and 4 to 5 million hectares being added to it annually, plantations are already well on the way to becoming the world's main source of wood. They are only a relatively minor producer at present, but this is only because most of the resource is still too young to utilize.

This example can do no more than make a point: it is far too simplistic to serve as a comprehensive guide to policy. The implied equivalence of needs with consumption is convenient, but misleading, unless the ineffective demand of unmet needs does cancel out the waste in effective demand. There is no reason for assuming it does: in contrast, there is much justification for believing it does not.

Most of the unmet need is for housing, especially in developing countries, and most of the wasteful consumption is of paper for packaging and administration, especially in developed countries.

The reason for rejecting the equivalence of unfilled need with wasted consumption, discussed above, is also substantiated on technical grounds. A demand for housing, effective or otherwise, does not necessarily imply a demand for wood. While wood is used in almost every type of housing, the extent to which it is used differs widely depending upon local building styles and techniques.

On the other hand, paper is largely wood-based and the wood requirements for various grades of paper are determined within fairly narrow limits. Hence, if the need for paper in developing countries and the excess use of it in developed countries could be estimated, this could provide the information necessary for fairly reliable estimates of roundwood requirements. An idea of the unfilled need for paper could be gained from demographic data and educational norms, but 'wasteful' or 'excessive use' is a different – and highly subjective – matter. What appears to be excessive or wasteful from a final consumer's point of view could legitimately be regarded by producers as necessary to the success of their businesses. Who is to say which view should take precedence?

Furthermore, the two supposedly compensating end uses operate in incompatible time-scales. Estimates of excessive use or unfilled needs for paper would likely be an annual quantity. In comparison, the wood requirement for housing is more of a once-and-for-all quantity. For the two to be comparable, a period over which the housing need was to be filled would have to be selected.

The most decisive grounds for disbelieving the equivalence assumption lie, however, in the differing natures of the wood required by housing and paper manufacturing. These two uses compete for similar types of wood on only a very limited scale. Logs suitable for sawnwood can be used in pulp production, but the reverse does not apply. Most of the roundwood suitable for pulping is too small, crooked or defective to be used also as sawnwood for housing. Pulpwood can be used for wood panels such as particle and fibre boards, but these panels are only partial substitutes for sawnwood in housing.

The differences in roundwood specifications are almost entirely technical. Interaction with economic factors can modify them, but only within narrow technical bounds. Little else can legitimately be taken into account, and certainly not the underlying moral distinction between socially responsible and irresponsible uses.

What emerges is the possibility that more may be gained by analysing the need for wood directly in very specific categories of roundwood, which are correlated with a finer set of end-use types than those usually adopted for global macro-projections.

This will not dispose of the 'need versus consumption' issue. What this approach might do, however, is to simplify the means by which an answer might be reached, by working forwards from wood production instead of backwards from wood consumption.

How this might come about can be illustrated by the following summary of the forest products sector. About half of the roundwood produced at present goes directly into final end uses such as fuelwood, poles, posts and pit props, without much in the way of processing. The remainder has to go through several processing and handling stages before it reaches the final users in housing, paper, furniture or any of the several thousand other items made with wood. Consider, however, how roundwood products can be reduced to three basic categories – logs, pulpwood and fuelwood – with the distinctions between them depending primarily on dimension and shape. **Logs** tend to be longer, larger, straighter, more symmetrical and derived from more species than **pulpwood**, which in turn is straighter than **fuelwood** and with fewer defects in wood quality. **Poles** might thus be regarded as superior, though smaller, logs; and **posts** as a superior and more durable form of pulpwood.

A few indicative examples show how the approach could work out. The technical rotation for plantation-grown logs ranges from ten years for some tropical softwoods, to thirty to forty years for some of the faster-growing temperate softwoods and higher quality tropical species, to sixty years or more with slower-growing temperate species. Mean annual increments range from 8 to 30 m^3 per hectare. An immediate expansion of the current global plantation rate by an extra one million hectares annually, using species concentrated towards the higher end of the increment range, would add 100 million m^3 a year continually to the world's wood supply from early in the next century. This would increase to over 600 million m^3 a year before the end of its second decade.

In other words, an increase of no more than 20 per cent in the present rate of plantation establishment would permit sustained consumption up to 60 per cent greater than the present level. (There is some margin allowed in these indicative calculations, in that the rates of increase in consumption of each of the three categories of roundwood are rather higher than those recorded in recent times. The probability of a steady increase in yield increments as research is translated into improved plantation management allows a further margin, but of uncertain magnitude. Both the research and its application are more likely to be market-oriented than driven by social needs.)

Thus fairly modest additions to the world's plantation programme should meet any greater need for sawnwood which might be associated with improved living standards in developing countries over the same time. Moreover, an addition to the plantation programme on that scale would add 40 million to 500 million m^3 of pulpwood as a by-product of management for log production, plus 20 million to 150 million m^3 of sawmilling residues suitable for wood pulp or reconstituted wood panels.

This means that if wood consumption in paper manufacturing were to increase at an average of 2 per cent per annum, much of the additional wood demand could be met as a by-product of plantations grown to produce logs.

A similar estimate in terms of fuelwood or pulpwood as the main product would give much the same answer: increasing needs, even if needs are considerably greater than consumption, for either fuelwood or pulpwood can be covered by a fairly modest increase in afforestation rates. The productivity of plantation is great enough that to meet any probable increase in the consumption of wood as a result of needs being met would present no great technical difficulty. The critical issue would then be the local constraints to afforestation.

There are, however, some obvious qualifications to the above indicative calculations. For a start, the comparisons are global. Regional, national and local balances are sure to differ quite markedly – and plantations are more likely to be developed and expanded where comparative advantages can be realized, rather than where the needs are greatest. In those circumstances, trade could not be relied upon to correct any more than a fraction of the local imbalances. Changes in trade and aid policies more radical than anything currently proposed would be needed to make any real difference. The effect of global comparisons is probably, therefore, to underestimate the scope of the plantation programmes needed in practice.

A second qualification is that not all the wood required can be grown in plantations. If wood requirements or consumption were simply a matter of quantities in the three roundwood categories, there would be no problem. But the ecology of some species producing special timbers is such that they cannot be established in open or line plantations; or they must be grown on such a long rotation, or with such complex management, that the plantation system may not be appropriate or efficient. The quantities concerned are not great, but by virtue of their specialized and high-value end uses and the limited substitution possibilities, they have a disproportionately high economic potential. Plantations can, at present, do little towards the continuation of their supply.

Such qualifications modify the overall conclusion a little, but do not alter it. They may mean that **to sustain, over the next century at least, the expected total (and increasing) world consumption of roundwood for all uses except some speciality timbers, the rate of planting worldwide might have to be 30 per cent higher than the present rate** (rather than 20 per cent) to cover the spatial distribution anomalies and to allow some capacity to meet the (currently) ineffective demand.

The device of switching the focus from predicted needs to the productive potential of plantations does get round the difficulties inherent in the question 'how much wood do we need?'. However, plantations, supplemented by sustainably-managed natural forests for certain products, do have the potential to meet the world's needs for wood, virtually regardless of how those needs might develop.

BOX 4.1

'Silvibusiness': corporate involvement in plantations – ideas for sustainable practice

Wood use in industry is high. Capital costs for industrial wood processing can be very large; a competitive pulp mill supplying the export market can cost US$900 million. Consequently, and given the dominance of major corporations in industry, there is much competition to provide industry with continuous, high quality, uniform supplies of wood at low cost and in large quantities. It is not, therefore, surprising that corporations, especially those directly involved in wood-using industries, have been increasing their involvement in plantations.

In industrialized countries, the consumption *per caput* of all major forest products is three and a half times that of a developing country, and so industrial wood demands can be said to have increased with prevalent patterns of development (Arnold 1991). Corporate plantations as yet account for only a small proportion of supplies. Clearly, there is major potential for corporations to increase their involvement and especially to increase the efficiency of wood supply.

Plantations offer many advantages over natural forests for industry, particularly their greater abilities to:

- **select the forest location**, and therefore to take advantage of local climate and soil (the most critical factors for tree productivity), as well as local infrastructure, transport and labour opportunities;
- **protect the boundaries and control the use** of plantations
- **predetermine fibre supply characteristics** through species/ variety selection and management;
- **apply 'industrial' techniques**, and regulate inputs and outputs in circumstances of bulk demand and imperatives for efficiency.

The government forestry sector, in developing countries in particular, has been generally inefficient at realizing the advantages of plantations. In almost all state-run plantations in Africa, the government has failed to make a profit (World Bank 1991). In contrast, the World Bank has

---

recognized that such investment decisions are better taken by enterprises and individuals in competition with each other and with the
outside world. There is ample evidence of thriving private-sector
plantation development in Europe, Latin America, Asia and North
America (although little as yet in Africa – Asibey 1991). Indeed,
throughout the world, governments have recognized the potential of the
private sector and commonly offer tax concessions for private afforess-
tation.

There are many opportunities to improve competitiveness in plantation forestry through new and more efficient technology, production
management and marketing. There is considerable immediate scope in
developing countries, where the level of mechanization is low and much
technology is inefficient and out of date – yet where there are locational,
environmental and labour advantages. Corporations may be better able
than governments to increase efficiency and competitiveness and realize
comparative advantage. Several characteristics of good private sector
business, relative to governments, would account for this:

- close and effective control of assets, and high capital mobility
  (especially to transfer between countries);
- financial size and resilience; being able to undertake long-term
  investments;
- ability to maximize use of tax and financial incentives for forestry;
- ability to work competitively in the marketplace, and hence to
  improve the efficiency of resource allocation and use;
- adequate resources to take on rapidly the very large task of
  afforestation;
- opportunity to complement investments in other sectors, notably in
  agriculture and forest product-using industries, with plantation investments;
- relatively attractive employment, training and social development
  conditions;
- access to markets and market information;
- access to technology and research capability;
- management know-how to deal with market and other uncertainties,
  and to adapt accordingly;
- institutional longevity compared to many government regimes.

Major corporate plantation investments have been run by corporations
alone or in partnership with governments, but as yet there are only a few

examples of the private sector joining forces with local communities, through outgrower farm-forest schemes and joint plantation ventures. These demand a new approach to communities, of joint planning, joint investment, and joint management, for which precedents are still few. As Chapter 5 shows, however, such approaches will be increasingly necessary.

The better corporate plantations have provided a real terms earning power of between 4 and 20 per cent per year, compared with negative returns from many inefficient public-owned projects.

A number of large companies have long made plantation their principal business. Private forest industry is traditionally highly fragmented, with the largest company accounting for less than 5 per cent of global sales, although American companies dominate. There is a growing internationalization of corporate plantations, for companies in traditional supply areas seek to become involved in the low-cost wood-supply potential of emerging regions. Hence companies in the northern hemisphere – until recently the major suppliers of wood pulp – are investing in pulp plantations in the southern hemisphere, particularly Chile, Brazil and New Zealand.

Plantations can provide an effective complement to other corporate investments, especially in agriculture. Large agricultural concerns in the United States have planted extensive forest shelterbelts to protect grain fields from wind erosion. Tobacco companies in southern Africa have established fuelwood plantations for tobacco curing (finding them cheaper and more reliable than bringing in coal). Commercial farms in France grow poplars as part of the agricultural rotation.

There are other forward- and backward-linkages from forest plantations. Companies move backwards into e.g. the supply of nursery stock and forward into e.g. the manufacture of furniture and construction goods, pulp and paper. In practice, however, most businesses have moved backward from the final product into investment in forestry; this can greatly increase efficiency, for transport costs of raw material can often represent half the value of an exported log.

Increasingly, non-forestry companies have diversified into forest plantation. The Shell International Petroleum Company's diversification was spurred on by the 1970s' oil price rises, when possible wood biomass substitutes for oil-based energy and petrochemical feedstocks were being investigated. Increasingly, however, forestry as a long-term renewable resource-based industry has been recognized by Shell as a legitimate diversification in its own right for, as we have noted, there are many opportunities to improve efficiency and competitiveness in forestry. Plantations are compatible with Shell's core activities as they are resource-based, long-term in nature and international in scope. Since 1980, Shell has built up major plantation resources in five countries – particularly in the southern temperate zone, making a conscious attempt to set high environmental and social standards. However, it has inevitably run into public criticism in its learning process (e.g. Lohmann 1990).

Demands are emerging in the marketplace for 'sustainably produced' timber. Corporations are beginning to respond to this. Mather (1990) describes this as deriving from a shift from an 'industrial' perception of forestry, to a 'post-industrial' perception, where forests are seen as more than the source of timber. Where this is expressed in the market, the public in effect purchases a moral good as well as a physical item.

To ensure that private sector plantations are sustainable, corporations should aim for operations which successfully meet commercial objectives – for the corporation, the principal criterion – but which also form an integral and accepted part of the local society, economy and landscape. Plantation sustainability will principally be achieved through maintaining ecological processes, biological diversity, harvest at sustainable levels, and social acceptability. In an economic sense, plantations should add value and increase efficiency. Occasionally the provision of social and ecological benefits from forestry can earn income, because demand for them enters the marketplace, such as some recreation, water supplies and land reclamation.

Perhaps the most significant challenge is to integrate the social dimension into corporate plantation planning, implementation and monitoring (see Chapter 5). Too many corporate plantations have aroused antipathy on the part of local people. The corporate culture, with its timetables, budgets and procedures can be very different from local cultures. The key point is for the pertinent decision-making structures in both local communities and corporations to be identified, and equitable agreements struck. In drawing up agreements, the full range of benefits and costs associated with plantations needs to be assessed, and mechanisms developed to distribute them fairly and ensure appropriate authority and controls. Good communications are essential to this process, as is a genuine commitment to it. In certain developing countries, at least, this will necessitate significant changes in corporate culture. Tokenism in public participation has proved to be inadequate.

Government roles must also be revised if the potential of corporate involvement in plantations is to be realized without undue cost.

Where appropriate, the production forestry sector should be transformed into a market area promoting sustainable development. Governments must therefore create conditions to ensure that plantation enterprises stay in business **but** do not reap an excessive proportion of forest rent. **Official incentives must create the signals for sustainable corporate practices:**

- ensure business access to the right kind of land – which entails neither compulsory acquisition (adverse social impacts) nor the clearing of natural forests (adverse environmental impacts);
- provide clear tenure, and leases of appropriate length, within effective land-use zones, to avoid conflicts with agriculture and other competing uses of land;
- foster an appropriate balance of control between the corporate developer and local communities;
- provide a stable fiscal and economic climate (low inflation, protection from high interest rates and undue taxes on land, stability in interest rates and taxes, stability of the market, price and trade conditions);
- recognize the 'lumpiness' of returns to plantations in taxation policy;
- provide clear performance-related regulations of conduct; based on e.g. the International Tropical Timber Organization standards for sustainable plantation management, adapted to reflect local criteria of sustainability.

Existing policy frameworks for plantations are generally more robust in western industrialized countries. Yet tropical countries have a comparative advantage for perennial crops such as trees – which can grow all year round at very high growth rates in warm conditions, and which require less cultivation of erodible soil than annual crops. Efforts by tropical country governments to create policy frameworks for sustainable corporate plantations would appear to offer potentially high rewards.

S.B.

Sources:
Arnold, J.E.M., *Long term trends in global demand for and supply of industrial wood*, Oxford Forestry Institute, 1991.
Asibey, E.O., *Development of private forest plantations to reduce pressure on natural forest in sub-Saharan Africa*, AFTEN Working Paper, 1991.

Lohmann, L., 'Commercial tree plantations in Thailand: deforestation by any other name', *The Ecologist* vol. 20 no.1, 1990.

Mather, A.S., *Global Forest Resources*, London: Belhaven Press, 1990.

Schmidheiny, S., and Business Council for Sustainable Development, *Changing Course: A Global Business Perspective on Development and the Environment*, Cambridge: MIT Press, 1992.

World Bank, *Forestry development: a review of Bank experience*, 1991.

BOX 4.2
Corporate plantations aiming for sustainability: Aracruz Celulose

Natural forests in Espirito Santo and Bahia on the Brazilian coast have been heavily exploited by farmers, charcoal makers, loggers and ranchers for decades. By the late 1960s, many lands had been left eroded or abandoned, and many local people were consequently impoverished and unemployed. Virtually no reforestation had taken place.

Aracruz Celulose S.A., with government support, took control of much degraded land within the tattered fragments of natural forest, and has established major *Eucalyptus* plantations. In doing so, it has begun to improve the local environment and social conditions. Its operation has been profitable, and has recently been greatly expanded. Aracruz is now one of Brazil's leading companies, with 1991 sales of over US$300 million, much from sales of kraft paper. It is now the world's largest producer of *Eucalyptus* pulp.

In the 1960s, species trials on the degraded land indicated the suitability of *Eucalyptus*, and an integrated development plan was prepared for 203,000 hectares. Aracruz claims to have conserved the 27 per cent of this area that was still covered with natural forest, and in addition planted 1.5 million native trees and 60,000 fruit trees to foster an increased bird population. Planting within the natural forest mosaic was also believed to reduce disease and pest risks in the *Eucalyptus* crop.

The first plantations were established in 1967 using locally-obtained *Eucalyptus* seed, but soon seed supplies were being introduced from other countries. These were employed in a tree improvement programme that yielded gains of up to 200 per cent in mean annual increment over the original introductions. Twenty-three per cent less wood was required per tonne of pulp. Aracruz's major breakthrough came in 1979, when vegetative propagation techniques permitted the development of disease-resistant strains with a minimum of side branching; propagated rooted cuttings being planted out and grown on a seven-year rotation. One hundred different clones are used and, to reduce the potential risks associated with a relatively narrow genetic resource base, the company has decided never to plant more than 26 ha with any one clone.

Aracruz runs a major kraft pulp mill, which was among the first in Latin America to adopt the relatively clean cell-membrane process. Ninety per cent of the mill's energy requirements are met from waste wood and bark. All the wood for the mill is said to be cut from Aracruz's forests or supplied by local growers – to whom Aracruz extends credit and distributes nine million free *Eucalyptus* seedlings every year. Soil fertility is monitored, nutrients are added when required, and tractors and lumber-handling equipment have been adapted to prevent soil compaction.

The chairman of Aracruz says that '*Eucalyptus* is a complement to, and not a substitute for, [natural] forests'. He is keen to point out that the plantations did not replace indigenous forests, but instead replaced a thoroughly degraded environment; and that Aracruz did not marginalize people but created employment. Since eighty per cent of production is exported, he sees his current challenge as better informing the 'green' Western consumer's preference for recycled paper; the virtues of paper produced from sustainable plantation forestry are not widely appreciated.

Aracruz would contend that it is possible to run a profitable operation whilst taking account of environmental and social factors. Clearly, the good growing conditions and low opportunity costs for the land (and labour) have been significant. As yet, however, the full economic costs and benefits of the Aracruz operatrion, including externalities, have not been assessed. A full and independent study could prove extremely fruitful.

S.B.

Sources:
Burley, J. and Ikemori, Y.K., 'Tropical forest production: the impact of clonal propagation technology' in *Towards an Agro-industrial Future*, Royal Agricultural Society of England Monograph Series No. 8, 1988.
Schmidheiny, S. and Business Council for Sustainable Development, *Changing Course: A Global Business Perspective on Development and the Environment*, Cambridge: MIT Press, 1992.
Lamb, C., 'Chopping Down Rainforest Myths', London: *Financial Times* 8th January, 1992.

CHAPTER 5

WHAT ABOUT THE PEOPLE?

Elaine Morrison and Stephen M.J. Bass

This chapter considers the interactions of plantations with society, and the ways in which the perceptions, needs and rights of local people may best be taken into account to achieve sustainable development. Current plantation approaches are reviewed with respect to mechanisms for participation, and recommendations are made for dialogue between local people and plantation developers at all stages. The ways in which local people may be represented and the means of information exchange are considered. The chapter concludes with recommendations for achieving appropriate balances of control such that commercial, social, cultural and associated environmental objectives are realized.

The social politics of plantations

Social structures

Communities are not homogeneous units – they are riddled with hierarchies, conflicts and contradictions. Superimposed upon traditional social structures, there may be 'new' structures such as local government, resource user groups. The interactions between them can have strong bearings on the success of plantations. Especially significant is the prevalence of government in forest ownership and forestry regulation, and its interactions with local systems.

Community structures determine who is involved in decision-making, how the decisions will be made, and whose interests will be favoured. Inequalities tend to be perpetuated or exaggerated. For example, in Tamil Nadu the democratically elected *Gram Sabhas* (village councils) are usually composed of high-caste, influential members of the community: lower-caste and poorer members are not represented and are not necessarily favoured in decisions affecting the community (Rogaly 1991). In most traditional hierarchical social systems 'the work gets done, the risk-spreading, exchanging and sharing take place, but not (necessarily) according to egalitarian principles' (Bennett quoted in Griffin 1988). Hence what might simply appear to an outsider as 'corruption' may, in fact, be a socially acceptable system of relationships, such as friend and family obligations and flattery involving unequals.

Perceptions and motivations

Only foresters are concerned with trees as economically productive organisms yielding a few physical products through manipulation according to an optimum mix of scientific and economic controls. Other people are more concerned with the many functions or meanings associated with trees – from the traditional and/or subsistence concerns (food, fuel, shelter, decoration, spirit homes, and sources of pests and diseases) to the modern imperatives of biodiversity conservation and recreation. Such functions, and thus the perception of the value of trees, will vary according to the social group, but all tend to have their roots in forest diversity. These values can rarely be replaced in their entirety by uniform plantations.

Clashes between perceptions of forests are especially acute in periods of transition, such as when new technologies are introduced, and when there are very rapid changes in the quantity of trees, e.g. major deforestation or afforestation schemes. In the tropics today, many such transitions are especially acute; the perception of cash equivalence of trees and forests tends to dominate where cash economies are developing and where cash is short. This clashes with traditional perceptions and values (such as sacred groves, where trees are valued, but not in cash terms) and it results more usually in deforestation than afforestation. Labelling forests and trees as 'resources' through economic activity removes the protective identity established through myth and custom, and opens them to exploitation.

With the development of a plantation, however, local people will be faced with the sudden introduction of a new set of circumstances, which is explainable locally only by reference to existing belief systems and values. Sensitivity to the possible impacts on the part of an industrial developer of plantations is essential. But the common attitude that 'perceptions must be changed' to secure a place for plantations in society must itself be changed. Often plantation forestry is **already** acceptable to a majority of individuals, albeit for reasons different to those of an industrial developer. The problem, however, is that local institutional and government structures, economic or policy signals, and the whims of certain leaders, may not permit plantations.

An illustration of the variety and clash of perceptions is found in the large-scale industrial plantation of exotics. The perceived role of exotics is strongly influenced by local myth – the way in which a group explains the unknown, for example, by attributing false properties to an exotic species. During an assessment of social attitudes to a proposed *Eucalyptus* plantation in Thailand, local people expressed a fear that *Eucalyptus* gives off a 'poison gas' which burns the ground, and that fallen leaves would be poisonous to nearby crops and to fish, should the leaves fall into streams (Sargent 1990). The perception of exotic species, possessing attributes different from those which are locally expected of trees, may extend to vehement antipathy. This is in marked contrast to the esteem in which commercial growers hold such species, but may be quite justified given that each group has different needs and expectations of the forest.

There may also be sharp differences in perception of exotics between different groups at the local level. In the state of Bihar in India, farmers had opted for *Eucalyptus* on settled, secure farmlands, perceiving the tree as a good source of income. However, tribal communities depend largely upon natural forests for food, medicines, fruits, timber and firewood, and have opposed efforts to plant *Eucalyptus* in favour of the traditionally dominant species, *Shorea*. They see *Shorea* as a culturally important tree, and a highly valuable source of food and fodder: in contrast they perceive exotics as worthless, and a barrier to access to natural forests. It is worth noting that these *Eucalyptus* plantations were established supposedly for 'social' benefit (Caufield 1985). Worldwide, the perceived poor ecological performance of *Eucalyptus* has been used by the poor and landless as a symbol of other grievances: against government, 'top-down' planning, and the appropriation of common land.

The conflict arising from differing perceptions of trees has become a social syndrome of plantation forestry worldwide. In extreme cases it has led to deforestation: developers may clear natural forest which they perceive as valueless, and communities may burn plantations which they perceive as harmful.

But perceptions and attitudes change, and exotic species are by no means universally decried by the 'public'. In the proposed *Eucalyptus* plantation in Thailand, some local people, although sceptical, were willing to try growing *Eucalyptus* themselves, attracted by the potential income. There have been similar experiences with *Eucalyptus* plantations in Spain and Portugal. One of the greatest challenges to the plantation developer is identifying and responding to differing – and changing – perceptions.

Economic incentives for plantations today are generally driven by the industrial sector, which purchases large quantities of uniform material for cash. The degree to which plantations may be accepted by the local community (and integrated into the local economy) will therefore depend in part on local peoples' attitudes to the cash economy and commerce. Certain cultures have an aversion to being in debt; others associate entrepreneurship with dissidents or unfavoured minorities, and so are reluctant to enter into commercial forestry relationships. In these instances, the availability of subsidized credit for forestry may be no incentive at all.

Yet there will generally be a latent – if not fully expressed – incentive to commercialize. Indeed, Arnold (1991b) shows that the economic imperative is high almost everywhere, and Foley and Barnard (1985) find that 'the commercial incentive is often the strongest stimulant to tree growing'. This incentive might be a job on the plantation, land rental income, a share of commercial proceeds, or agricultural assistance from a plantation developer. In plantation outgrower schemes, landowners and farmers of all types have proved themselves just as responsive to changes in wood markets as corporations.

Finney (quoted in Lamb 1990) describes two factors which predispose societies to commercialize:

Internal to a society there may be **cultural preadaptations** which are conducive to commercial activity. They include an emphasis on individual achievement, a cultural focus on wealth and its exchange, and systems where status can be achieved through an individual's own efforts.

External to a society there may be **economic preconditions** which make the adoption of commercial activities feasible, attractive and profitable to the people concerned. Such factors include suitable transport systems, marketing and technical advice.

There are many differences in the motivations for involvement in plantations between richer and poorer landowners/farmers, and between the landless and the unemployed. They face different scarcities and constraints, and have differing attitudes to risk and uncertainty. Good rates of return, grants and tax concessions for forestry generally motivate the richer landowners/farmers. If poorer smallholders are to plant trees in commercially usable quantities, however, they may have to change the pattern of their already intensive land use, and to finance their daily needs while the trees mature. They have lower abilities to bear risks, and weaker access to credit. Consequently, high, quick and reliable returns from forestry, and secure jobs on the plantation, may provide stronger motivations.

Local motivations may be very complex in situations where land tenure is in flux, where markets for forestry products are changing but may not be well-established, and where there is a climate of speculation. Such conditions prevail today.

Rights to land and resources

The land on which plantations are established is often used by local people, and their rights to land and resources are of paramount import-ance in planning plantations. Tiffen and Mortimore (1990), referring to agricultural plantations, believe the legislative framework of land and labour laws to be more important than the colour of the political system in determining whether the plantation mode of management is possible.

Tenure systems can be highly complex and can both encourage and discourage plantations. Tenure indicates the power relationships within a society, and defines rights to land or trees. Tenurial rights can be redefined, passed on by inheritance, sold and recast. Tenurial matters in forestry can be complicated by separate tenure for land and trees; by changing according to the seasons; and by ownership changes over the long life of forest crops. Tenure is not easily manipulable, however, and it is difficult to isolate it from the overall power structure.

Tenurial matters may also be complicated by the conflict of customary rights with rights supported by law: the formal ownership structure may not necessarily reflect who actually makes the decisions over land use. Customary tenure may pre-date official land codes, and local interpre-tations of ownership, tenure and rights may dominate in practice: the distance from communal lands, the status of a particular landowner, and local precedent can all establish differences from the norm.

Where formal tenure has been allocated to local people, it does not always recognize and secure equitable rights for the landless and weaker social groups who may depend on forest resources. Powerful groups have exploited poorer user groups through the formal tenure system.

In tropical areas, governments have tended to enforce extreme forms of forest tenure, i.e. nationalization or privatization, ignoring the existence and benefits of tenure that lie between these extremes.

Formal systems of tenure may permit, and even encourage, unsustain-able use of natural forests, for many are based on historical imperatives to turn forest land into farmland. They provide a framework for perverse policy, fiscal and economic signals to have their effect, resulting in land booms and speculation, short-term resource abuse and the marginalization of people who have traditional claims to land.

Although secure tenure is a significant precondition for the rehabilitation of degraded land and forests, it is frequently not obtained in such areas. Similarly, land tenure in the remoter lands commonly made available by governments for plantation forestry is often characterized by a lack of formal registration, and by conflict of traditional tenure schemes with codified tenure.

The impacts of plantations on society

Because plantations form part of local land use and livelihood systems, they themselves help to shape local communities and local economies. As a land-intensive activity that takes place over many years, plantation forestry inevitably means that alternative land uses have to be foregone, and therefore has extensive social costs and benefits. The question of how to sort out the best mix of uses, and who should make the decisions, is critical – but it has frequently not been explored. The impacts of a plantation on people will depend on:

- the size of the plantation;
- the plantation's boundary configuration with respect to adjacent land uses;
- the rate of plantation establishment;
- the particular type and objectives of the plantation, especially the species used, and their familiarity to the community;
- the degree of lifestyle change that the plantation objectives entail, notably through employment and changes in social benefits;
- the relative economic, political and legal power of local people and the developer.

Plantations will have impacts upon the following:

1. **The local land-use pattern** and the **configuration of the plantation** with other land-use systems: the precise pattern of plantations in land use will determine many potential social benefits – such as watershed and soil conservation, windbreaks, transport infrastructure and welfare facilities.

   Once established, plantations lock up land for many years, during which economic change and development could otherwise favour different land uses. In many regions which are short of land, an intricate framework of highly intensive land uses is required, and plantation schemes may be inappropriate if they are too large. Plantations may also take away common land that is important for subsistence use and for allocation to future generations. This has direct effects on adjacent land: Chambers *et al.* (1989), referring to India, quote a World Bank document which admits that:

neither private nor public plantations have been very effective in reducing local village pressure on nearby forest lands. This failure is due primarily to the commercial orientation of plantations on public lands and failure to plan social forestry operations in the context of local land-use patterns.

2. **Socially useful services** like water supply and landscape; and **products** like fuel, fruit, nuts, fodder and game: plantations established on deforested or degraded land may greatly increase useful services and benefits – even if initially there is an impoverished period when the plantation is young. The availability of fuelwood from single-species plantations (as brash, thinnings, or final harvest) can increase their social value, especially in developing countries where up to 90 per cent of all energy used is in the form of fuelwood. However, single-species/ purpose plantations, entailing loss of diversity and access, usually do not meet local people's needs. The exotic forest species which are silviculturally favoured tend to produce fewer products, are frequently poorer fuelwoods and fodder sources and may be inferior in durability. Where resources shift from producing locally used products to 'exported' wood products, benefits are transferred from local people to those profiting from the exotic species. Plantations of exotic species are also likely to support a smaller range of indigenous flora and fauna; and to create alien landscapes.

Because so many plantations aim at a very limited set of values, they usually exclude values which are identified as important by local communities, e.g. for subsistence, medicinal, environmental or cultural reasons. These losses are rarely costed in investment analysis – usually because the cost is not borne by the plantation developer, and few of the 'minor' products are commercially traded. Impacts may be especially negative if natural forests are cleared to make way for plantations (the cultural values thereby lost are as important as the more commonly-cited lost watershed, soil fertility and biodiversity values). Many social activities may be prejudiced by the effects of the plantation on water quality and quantity – hunting, fishing, gathering, drinking, etc. – as well as loss of cottage industries. Chambers *et al.* (1989) cite a recent study of areas in Orissa and Chattisgarh which were heavily forested a few decades back. With the removal of the local natural forest, the distance required to collect forest products multiplied severalfold.

3. **Incomes, equity and welfare**: rates of return of 15 to 25 per cent can be realized by small-scale farm plantations, under participatory forestry schemes supplying an industrial market. Plantations can thus have a positive impact, especially if there is a good continuity of income. For example, in Gujarat it has been profitable for farmers to produce fuelwood and poles on land that would otherwise have been planted with cotton and tobacco. Other plantation projects have increased welfare by providing infrastructure and facilities.

In remote areas, the introduction of a cash economy is beneficial only where it is adequate to increase net social benefits, compensating for the removal of a subsistence economy. Impacts have been negative when markets for forest products are not well established, are inaccessible, or where there is poor market information. For example in Vietnam, plantations have been established for social purposes, but have failed due to the lack of a good market for produce. A criterion of success for a plantation project in Papua New Guinea has been defined as 'a balance between the subsistence and cash economies, so that the standard of living is not jeopardized' (Lagercrantz 1981).

Where people outside the cash economy have been removed from the land, they have been forced to become producers and consumers in the modern economy. Yet economic niches have often not been available to poorer people, who have thus not been able to buy food. Social systems, that otherwise might have guaranteed them community largesse in the absence of a cash economy, have disintegrated (Lohmann 1990).

Where key subsistence and agricultural land is taken up for forestry, with resulting poorer food availability and nutritional status, reduced welfare has been well documented (e.g. by FAO 1989a). However, although food prices have been known to rise where plantations have replaced food crops (as in Karnataka), it is more common that plantations replace cash crops or natural forest/grassland.

Participation in plantation projects has generally been aimed at those who have land, or other powerful groups that are able to benefit from forestry development. In 1985, after ten years of government subsidies for Chilean forest plantations, it was determined that just three Chilean corporations accounted for 70 per cent of the planting grants, plantation area, and timber exports – a very uneven distribution of the costs and benefits of plantations (CODEFF 1991).

4. **Land tenure**: the process of establishing plantations can potentially act as a catalyst for clarifying ambiguous tenure, for redistributing land, and for securing usufruct rights for the landless.

However, there are many potentially negative impacts of plantations on tenure. Clarifying title without accompanying this with positive changes in tenure regulations can also encourage land speculation and increase landlessness. In communities where boundaries have never been drawn formally, afforestation can permanently exclude the less influential people who were tolerated before. They are cut off from the grazing land or firewood upon which they may be utterly dependent, or (as in Uttar Pradesh) from land which they had reserved for future distribution to the landless. Such exclusion is quite common, especially where no care has been taken to ascertain customary uses. It is, in fact, much more common than the conscious alienation of land for plantation development (Evans 1982).

Many plantation programmes run the risk of unwittingly converting common property resources into state-controlled resources. The 'lands available for plantation' may in fact be subject to all kinds of traditional tenurial pressures that are not immediately obvious. This is especially the case with common lands, where jurisdiction and usufruct rights are unclear.

In many (traditional) societies, concepts of freehold and transferring rights to a leaseholder – forms of land tenure which are familiar to plantation developers – do not exist. This can lead to confrontation when a landowner becomes dissatisfied with the use to which the land is being put. In Papua New Guinea, for example, this has necessitated continual negotiation on land use, and not just initial discussions at the beginning of a plantation project. Here, the failure of plantation proposals has been 'largely attributed to local people not wishing to see a permanent, and perhaps not particularly profitable, commitment of their land to state-mediated or external investment' (Sargent 1989). Plantation developers have consequently invested little in Papua New Guinea, except on state land, which covers only 1.3 per cent of the territory.

5. **Employment** is the commonest social benefit of industrial plantations.

Indeed, Chambers *et al.* (1989) consider plantation programmes to have seldom offered any participation beyond employment. Gregersen *et al.* (1989) note that 'commercialization of forestry is essential' in order to increase employment – implying that 'strict' social forestry is comparatively inadequate in this respect. Industrial forestry may also provide employment if it is closely associated with local forestry processing industries.

Plantation employment is only beneficial to local people if they do not become overdependent on forestry – and if it encourages job and skill creation in other sectors as well. Training local people, and continuity in employment, are essential parts of sustainable plantation development. In very marginal agricultural areas, forestry establishment can be more labour-intensive than agriculture – requiring between 70 man-days per hectare (afforestation on grassland) to 400 man-days per hectare (steep terrain). Yet forest management thereafter will provide only about 9 to 15 man-days per hectare every year.

In spite of the positive impacts cited above, very often plantation development results in a long-term net loss of employment – as in the areas of Chile where major plantations have been established (CODEFF 1991). This is also common in the densely-settled multi-crop agricultural areas of SE Asia whenever forestry replaces intensive agriculture and displaces rural workers.

Other disruptions result from: withdrawing work from other local activities; upsetting prevailing wage structures in relation to other industries; and withdrawing employment once major plantation establishment work is completed. If labour is imported for plantation schemes, there will be significant impacts on communities.

6. **Local infrastructure**: intensive infrastructure, notably roads and worker housing, is often required for plantations, especially in remote areas and in the tropics. Many large tropical plantations have made major investments in housing (often in 'forest villages' – such as Jari in Brazil, the Viphya plateau in Malawi and Usutu Forest in Swaziland); and also in shops, schools, clinics, recreational facilities, telephones, water supplies, farms managed for food production and transport. In other projects (e.g. in Minais Gerais, the Fiji Pine Commission plantations, and Shiselwini Forestry in Swaziland) housing is not provided but other welfare facilities have been offered, e.g. food rations, work clothing and health care.

The impact of intensive infrastructure may be very conspicuous.

Roads can make the most dramataic impacts; they reduce isolation, opening up a range of new economic possibilities, increasing exposure to other cultures, and broadening access to government and to services.

Roads and facilities – rather than plantation products as such, or the possibility of employment – have sometimes provided the main incentive for local people to become involved in plantations. They can make significant improvements to the local quality of life, allowing agriculture and other local economic activities to diversify. But this is only the case if infrastructure is freely available to the whole community for a wide range of its needs, and is based on local needs and norms.

Facilities established by plantation developers have sometimes not built on social and cultural norms and trends, e.g. Fordlandia in Brazil. A major plantation project, with its associations of limitless financial resourses, can raise all kinds of expectations in a community, and undelivered expectations can damage relationships between the community and the plantation developer. A common disappointment is the 'agroforestry' component of certain plantation projects such as outgrower schemes. In practice, agroforestry assistance provided to farmers has often been minimal, or it has been withdrawn by developers wherever agricultural activities are deemed inconvenient for forestry.

Current approaches to social issues

Most plantation programmes now include a degree of participation. However, the interpretation of what participation really means varies greatly. According to Chambers, 'I manage, you participate' has been the dominant underlying principle behind government projects in India (Chambers et al. 1989). Elsewhere, even projects which have sought to identify local needs, aspirations and possibilities have done so more on the basis of the views of planners and others from outside, than of local people. Issues to do with people are still termed 'social constraints' by foresters. The important question is – participation for whose benefit, and on what terms?

In India and Nepal, participation now tends to take place within joint forest management arrangements. Management is practised by specific user groups rather than by the village or *panchayat* as a whole, and is particularly successful where the user group has secure tenure. The missing ingredient has been effective agreements between village groups and local representatives of the government, but recent experience suggests that such groups and working arrangements can mature in a relatively short period (Arnold 1991b).

In contrast, working with whole communities has been more difficult than with individual farms or other private lands. The village forest – except in parts of China, Republic of Korea and Nepal – has not worked too well. This is partly because ownership, the rights to cut and manage, and the distribution of costs and benefits are rarely clearly defined within communities, and internal pressures may undermine or overwhelm agreed systems of local control. Success with joint management has also been impeded by the reluctance or inability of forest departments to devolve responsibility, especially where they fear loss of control over the timber resource.

The participation of women may be restricted by social norms which mean that they are often less active in the cash economy. Consequently, women may be motivated by the availability of fuelwood and other forest products which are valuable in the subsistence economy. The removal of access to such resources is not normally adequately compensated. However, as experience in the Northern Areas of Pakistan shows, commercial forestry – and especially associated forest nurseries – can present income-earning possibilities for women who have no source of cash income (Bass 1987).

In some instances, women and children have formed a majority of the labour force, particularly in nursery work but also in plantations, e.g. in India and Brazil. But their involvement may be attributed partly to antisocial reasons – as in the major afforestation of Kenya, where the poor status of women and children meant that wage rates were very low compared to those of men. Positive reasons for involvement, their specialized needs, knowledge and roles in contributing to the quality of development, are rarely investigated, even in many participatory forestry projects.

Many problems arise from outsiders' misunderstandings of local motivations. These may be manifest in an unthinking desire to replace local people with others whom outsiders understand and appreciate better, i.e. further outsiders. Local cultural attitudes to work are important, and often leisure is highly valued. Evans (1982) cites one of the main labour 'problems' of the Usutu Pulp Company as the Swazi's 'preference for leisure rather than high wages'.

Rather than condemning people as unmotivated, it is more constructive to identify local motivations and predispositions for plantation forestry and to strive to work with them. The challenge is now for foresters to explore unfamiliar landscapes of human motivation and doubt, myth and creativity, and of like and dislike (Burch 1987).

Government procedures in many countries do not encourage this. Rather, governments may circumvent negotiations with communities to secure lucrative forestry contracts, and may adopt blunt measures to establish plantations – such as resettlement and compulsory acqui-sition. In the Philippines, traditional forest dwellers, and those that have lived in state forests even for several generations, are classed as squatters, and resettlement is an automatic part of many plantation investments. Yet resettlement is not in the interests of industrial plantation developers, who lose a potential work force, gain disgruntled neighbours, and may have to pay the costs of resettlement.

People have also been moved without resettling. In Buriran Province, Thailand, the government has encouraged private companies to rent National Reserve Forests, in order to grow *Eucalyptus* for meeting the huge (predominantly Japanese) demand for woodchips. 'Squatters' have been pushed out of these reserves, and are no longer able to supplement their income from common land forests. The people are increasingly fighting back, however, for access to common land and for the right to veto industrial forestry operations (many sources cited in Lohmann 1990). PICOP presents a more positive approach to 'squatters' (see Box 5.2), as do recent developments in Kenya and Tanzania.

The trend towards government ownership of forest lands – which cuts across the subtle, overlapping, traditional tenure systems, and often attempts to ignore them – has tended to bias against private forestry investments. Many local people fear that if land is afforested it will be lost to the government, or people will be deprived of access. In Haiti, rural people have been told by extension workers that all trees belong to the government, and anyone cutting trees would be punished. Although the intention was to protect trees, the effect was the reverse; people deforested further, because they assumed the government's interest in trees would lead to the expropriation of all afforested land.

Governments are therefore faced with fundamental political choices, notably:

• in economic planning, priority may be given either to the plantation sub-sector, because of its economic importance; or to tackling popula-tion growth, land shortage and unemployment by consolidating the smallholder sector;
• a choice must be made, or a balance struck, between nationalization, the

encouragement of foreign investment, and the promotion of local investment in the plantation sub-sector.

(Tiffen and Mortimore 1990)

In the past, industrial plantation developers exercised dominant control and concentrated on the large-scale planting of exotic tree species for just one type of product. This approach requires a well-organized, stable system of intervention if it is to thrive – something which it has appeared to developers to be easier to achieve if the plantation is totally under developer control. However, such an approach has been unsustainable in the longer term. Political backlashes, labour problems, illicit fellings, vandalism and even sabotage have resulted. The challenge now is to pursue both the interests of local people and the interest of a commercial developer, establishing a balance of control.

However, before trying to share control routinely with local people, there may be a need to strengthen local organizations, as local management should be in a fit state to participate successfully.

Many traditional forms of common property resource management have weakened or collapsed under increasing population pressure, greater commercialization and technological change. It is therefore necessary to look at the potential for sustainable contemporary forms of common property management.

In India, effective functioning communal management systems tend to have: use regulations which are evolved and enforced locally; simple individual rules and an ability to change these rules to meet new challenges; benefits allocated by the community to reflect the realities of the community structure; and management focused on products of importance to local people (Arnold 1991b).

Problems tend to be pronounced where access to forest products is combined with rights to cultivate land – such as on tree pattas (leases) in India, stewardship contracts in the Philippines, STK land entitlement certificates in Thailand (whereby rights to use of the land may be inherited but not transferred), and the forest management agreements between the State Forest Corporation and groups of farmers practising taungya on forest land in Java.

The discipline of 'participatory forestry', comprising e.g. 'social forestry' and 'community forestry' has developed to address situations where social needs are paramount. Participatory forestry serves local needs through actively involving the beneficiaries in all forestry activities, and in sharing benefits. Since the late 1970s, the notion of forestry as a 'social service' has become predominant in many countries' forest policies. Over the past fifteeen years in India, US$400 million has been spent on participatory forestry programmes, mainly on private lands (Poffenburger 1990). Official aid policy has moved away from supporting industrial plantation developments in favour of participatory forestry, and plantations for social benefit have increased more than all other forms of plantation. The World Bank's reappraisal of lending in the forestry sector concluded that forestry's major contribution to development is 'its impact on raising the incomes of indigenous people' (Spears 1978, quoted in Evans 1982).

Overall, the experience of recent years reveals a number of plantation types that can be beneficial to local people and commercial interests alike:

- **industrial plantations providing a proportion of the harvest to local people** with a clear, agreed distribution mechanism;
- **industrial plantations with multi-purpose trees** as a component, and guaranteed public/community access for fuel, fodder, mushrooms, honey, poles and other products;
- **small plantation blocks within a farm system**; usually as outgrower plantations (providing shelter, soil and water conservation and sources of income to the farmer);
- **silvi-pastoral systems** in which commercial wood production and local grazing are combined (management agreements being needed to protect trees from grazing);
- **agroforestry systems** in which wood production and agricultural crops are combined (but here long-term silvicultural/agricultural com-patibility must be ensured);
- **integral taungya systems**, where a large forest plantation development is built up by the careful phasing of many small operations. (The social impact is reduced by slowing the rate at which the land-use system or local ways of life are altered);
- **tree tenure forestry**, where landless or poor farmers establish plan-tations on state land allocated specifically for tree growing. Current examples are to be found in West Bengal, Rajasthan, Gujarat and Himachal Pradesh;
- **recreational/amenity forestry** – plantations that can accommodate walking, hunting, fishing, nature study, etc.

In general, multiple species/purpose plantations are more desirable for local people than current single-species/purpose plantations. However, apart from some taungya schemes, there are few industrial operations running multiple species/purpose plantations. Successful operations are likely to build upon traditional forestry techniques, or upon agroforestry systems of intercropping, underplanting or rotational cropping. 'Given the circumstances of rural societies and land scarcity prevalent in much of the non-industrial world, the integration of other crops with plantation forestry is likely to be the best means of successful plantation production in the future' (World Bank 1991, quoted in van Ginneken 1992). Further research in this area should therefore be fruitful.

Whatever type of plantation is chosen, the precise boundary configuration – the shape and size of the plantation with respect to neighbouring land uses – is most important. Plantation schemes have been far more acceptable locally when certain (often small) areas, such as rights of way, have been excised because of their social or cultural value, and when the plantation edge is designed to provide social or environmental benefits. Clearly, knowing where not to plant is as important as knowing where to plant. Indeed, this principle applies as much at global and national levels as in the plantation locality.

Representation, information exchange and democracy

Through the media and democratic movements, people have become more vocal in their condemnation of plantations which they percieve to be poor. The private sector has become wary of the political problems associated with industrial plantation development. With notable exceptions, this has influenced a recent decrease in corporate plantation investments (Johnson 1991). We may conclude that, although plantation policy is now more socially-oriented, the techniques, incentives and means to encourage socially- and culturally-sustainable plantations have been distinctly lacking.

What factors have led to such opposition? There are various agents of representation of local people's views, with greater or lesser degrees of authenticity. They include the people themselves, local, national, and international NGOs, local politicians and the media. Some agents can be powerful to the point of directly influencing policy: Chambers *et al.* describe:

a lobby of environmentalists, academics and members of the press who tend to see planting trees for economic gain in capital and cash as moral sin. People's participation, according to them, should mean planting trees for the next generation, or for meeting fuelwood and fodder needs of the people, or for supplementing agricultural production. A market orientation, in their view, harms the poor, as they are vulnerable to exploitation by middlemen, have little control over markets, and are likely to sell their trees for a song long before their optimal silvicultural and economic stage is reached. People's participation is also equated with arousing collective spirit among the community, which alone will ensure that the new wealth being created through the programme reaches the poor.

(Chambers *et al.* 1989)

The influence of this lobby on policy (in Chambers' example, in India) should not be underrated. Its views are readily accepted as defining desirable objectives, to the extent that contrary viewpoints may easily be branded as anti-poor. Both the authorities and environmental lobbies see rules and controls as solutions, and make blunt decisions such as the banning of tree cutting. Ironically, such rules can be self-defeating, as they also tend to discourage tree plantintg and protection (as in the Haitian example quoted earlier).

Paradoxically, the representation of local people's views may not be participatory, even though the agents of representation would likely condone extensive public participation. In fact, criticisms of plantations may come from areas remote from the plantation, such as international NGOs based in the west. This may, none the less, be valuable to the local people in societies with little freedom to express their views.

Criticism within developed countries is frequently directed at private interests and transnational companies owning and running plantations, particularly where these are Northern companies operating in Southern countries. The public believes that these companies are responsible for low wages, poor housing and social welfare, unjust land appropriation or other unacceptable practices (Tiffen and Mortimore 1990). Apologists for the 'modern plantation' have therefore been at pains to stress the indigenization of ownership in recent years, whether by nationalization or by sale and transfer. Although Western public opinion has accorded high priority to environmental criteria, plantations that are locally owned are less vulnerable to environmental criticism than are foreign-owned plantations.

The influence of the agents of representation upon public opinion can therefore be highly significant to the success or otherwise of the plantation. As with the participation of local people, involvement of NGOs and other representative groups at an early stage in plantation planning will reduce potential conflicts. Local agents of representation can greatly assist the developer by acting as intermediator, and can help in the necessary information exchange with local people. As the development progresses, NGOs can help to strengthen local groups and institutions, and provide them with market information.

The critical stance of national and international NGOs has catalysed the development of more appropriate plantation policies, even though mechanisms for implementing the policies may still be lacking. To this end, representation of local people's views by agents distant from the plantation have brought results directly helpful to local people. But however vocal the NGOs are, donors and governments are not yet predisposed to address land tenure and participation routinely.

Recommendations

The basis of participation

The recommendations presented here are concerned mainly with industrial plantations, requiring such levels of investment that government and/or corporate backing is essential.

Participation of local people in such plantations should generally build on an initial assessment of social structure, necessary to identify:

- the social groups which use forest resources and which may be interested in involvement in the plantation;
- the ability of different elements within these groups to become involved;
- the local political and economic power structure; systems and traditions used in cooperating and conflicting with other social groups, with government, and with business (the reallocation of resources to commercial ends and the introduction of a relatively powerful 'user group', the developer, can bring radical changes);
- community decision-making processes; leaders that make forest and land-use decisions; sources of motivation; incentives and disincentives for involvement in plantations;

- the 'agents of representation', if any, of the local people, and the measures required for comprehensive information exchange with them;
- formal tenure, and customary and overlapping tenure and claims;
- social, cultural and religious perceptions of trees, forests and plantations;
- traditional forest control systems.

In addition to users of the specific land in question, representatives of the entire community must be consulted. Special attention must be given to gender issues (Box 5.3). However, once local people's views are clear, a smaller number of contacts is desirable for continuing information exchange and negotiation.

Such assessments will provide information about the local community for the developer. However, unless there is a continued, two-way exchange of information between the community and the developer, hearsay and unrealistic expectations concerning the plantation may prevail. A high level of trust between communities and the developer is crucial, and the developer must ensure that communities have full information, including market, credit and financial information. Communities must then be given both the time and the opportunities to make decisions based on this information.

Carrying out participation

The developer's approach to participation will affect the results of any survey. Several potential difficulties must be faced:

Social/cultural analysis requires a holistic and participatory approach, very different from the reductionist and detached, technical and financial analyses with which developers are familiar.

The commonly-applied development appraisal methods tend to bias forestry appraisal teams against understanding social and cultural diversity. Such biases arise from teams staying near roads; visiting only in the post-harvest season; meeting only the influential and better-off, men rather than women, adopters rather than non-adopters, the active rather than the inactive; visiting areas where there are already projects as opposed to no projects; with politeness and protocol prejudicing against real inquiry. The bias is against meeting society as a whole, and against perceiving the full extent of social deprivation and inequality on the one hand, and cultural diversity on the other (Chambers 1986).

Finally, unfamiliar societies and cultures present many aspects that potentially could be examined, but not all are relevant. Wasteful research is all too possible.

These difficulties may partly be overcome by including local representation in the appraisal team and, rather than seeking total comprehensiveness, by adopting a strategic approach. Enough information should be gathered to incorporate people's perspectives and to make a common construct of local people's and the plantation developer's needs.

The management and decision-making styles and expertise of industrial forestry differ from traditional community methods and expertise. Where people are to be involved in plantations, it is important to integrate them. To achieve this, the plantation developer may wish to give a reasonable degree of management autonomy to a local staff office – in which local professionals are represented at management level, who can interpret and respond to local needs.

For consulting with communities in the field, local consultative mechanisms and styles, and local languages and media, should be most effective. Formal questionnaires, which imply officialdom and elicit evasive answers (see e.g. Griffin 1988), may result in misinterpretation of questions and biased responses. Informal techniques tend to work best in remote areas and in those communities which are not used to officials. They may not reveal accurate-looking results, but they can often yield better, quicker estimates than the spuriously accurate products of more formal methods.

Many of these techniques are included in participatory/rapid rural appraisal (P/RRA), a suite of methods which is ideal for assessing social factors. This collection of techniques is summarized in Box 5.1.

Other field participation techniques include: informal group discussion to expose differences in local perceptions, and later to assist consensus-building; confidential interviews; key informants (local counterparts to the appraisal team); formal workshops open to interested members of the public; sample surveys; and direct observation of behaviour (open to erroneous interpretation unless the observer is well trained).

In addition to field assessments, local literature in social sciences and humanities, and demographic and cadastral records, should also be consulted. The status of land tenure, both *de facto* and *de jure*, should be ascertained at an early stage; this will also help to tailor incentives for participation to the specific landowner/occupier.

Between them, these techniques should reveal the following information:

Demographics
- Population composition and dynamics
- Migration patterns and migration history
- Transmigration plans and programmes
- Educational levels and literacy

Social organization
- Social organization structure
- Local institutions and leadership
- Decision-making processes
- Distribution mechanisms
- Differentiated roles
- Social institutions regulating access to land and forest benefits

Socioeconomic (household) conditions
- Employment profile
- Income and subsistence patterns
- Household budget, time use (over day/year), energy needs
- The current level of commercialization of forestry

Land/tree tenure and use systems
- Land distribution and availability of land
- Ownership and possession of the land
- Rights of land allocation and use
- Security of land tenure
- Ownership, rights of use and security of tenure of trees
- Compensation mechanisms for withdrawn tenure and rights
- Current land use
- Cultural practices likely to hinder forestry, e.g. annual burning
- Household use of forest products
- Traditional/current land management systems, their sustainability and their productivity

Inputs
- Social opportunity cost of key inputs – especially water

Cultural and religious attributes
- Belief systems and attitudes concerning natural forests, trees, plantations and land use
- Cultural practices and customs concerning trees
- Perceptions of change and of agents of change

Incentive structures
- Economic (market)
- Social and cultural (non-market)

History
- How the above factors have changed over time; identifying the dominant forces behind these changes; conflicts over tenure; an examination of the local history of forest treatment

In collecting this information and entering into consultations, developers will inevitably need to clarify their social policy to government authorities. They will also need to determine how governments obtain land for plantations and deal with the social implications of this. Governments must usually be involved in settling tenurial matters; this should, of course, not be the responsibility of the plantation developer.

Frequently, formal government approval must be secured for the proposed roles of local people in plantation schemes, e.g. issuing community stewardship certificates for the management of land that is state property, or other documents of entitlement or agreement, as are commonly required in India (Poffenberger 1990). Formal documentation is often needed even if local people are only to be responsible for plantation protection.

In addition to inviting information from local people, participation involves the spread of information regarding the development to the local people, and its implications regarding their rights. The means of communication are many and varied. The television and video revolution has already reached rural areas in many developing countries, and can be expected to multiply in its impact in the 1990s. More traditional channels include radio, posters, speeches, newspapers, and handbills in local languages. The same message, received through different channels, gains in credibility and weakens the case of those who would challenge it. NGOs and other representatives of local people can help, acting as watchdogs, supporting poor and under-represented groups in securing their rights, and ensuring that information flow is uncorrupted.

Achieving a balance of control

Plantation operations should be able to meet commercial objectives successfully, whilst also forming an integral part of the local society, economy and landscape. This will necessitate an approach which treats social and cultural factors as seriously as economic and technical factors, at all stages of the plantation development process. The need for agreement between developers and local interests is so fundamental that plantation developers should be prepared to commit adequate time, expertise and funding to securing it.

Even if good relationships are established between plantation developer interests and local interests, tensions will remain inevitable: each party will seek to protect its respective investment. The balance of decision-making, control over the plantation, and the sharing of costs and benefits between local people and developer has to be agreed. However, there must also be room for shifting the balance to mutual benefit.

Local people will require significant control over the siting and running of plantations. Local people's land and resource rights and use are paramount, whether or not they are expressed formally, and must be respected. Exclusivity, transferability, divisibility, and enforceability of rights should be ensured (Binkley and Vincent 1990), for the plantation and its products need not necessarily remain in one ownership over the production period. Subject to local circumstances, **community control** is desirable for:

- **land allocation**: communities must have a veto in land allocation for plantations. This should extend to the precise definition of boundaries. Having done so, communities should rarely, however, have the power to withdraw land from plantations prior to an agreed date.
- **protecting the forest**: formal plantation protection plans can be supplemented, to advantage, by prevailing community rules and control systems.
- **employment and service contracts**: first options on jobs and contracts could go to qualified local people. Special arrangements might be made for preferential employment of the poor and landless. The highest applicable employment and health and safety standards should be assured.
- **marketing and distributing benefits locally**: the community should have preferential access to marketed products (at locally-acceptable prices) and usufruct rights.
- **infrastructure**: communities should be involved in infrastructure design and layout, particularly roads and welfare facilities.
- **technical guidance**: local guidance should be sought on species choice and management techniques. Access to local ecological knowledge can avoid many technical errors and reduce the amount of research needed.

- **research**: participatory research may help in outgrower schemes. Local people should be able to make their own adaptations.
- **monitoring and evaluation**: communities must have adequate opportunities and resources to contribute to formal, periodic evaluations of a plantation. They must also be able to make respresentations to an impartial third party, e.g. local government.

The **plantation developer** must be able to secure the plantation's commercial viability over the long time horizons associated with forestry. Some factors must inevitably remain under the principal control of the developer:

- **inputs** that have to be of consistently high quality and regularly supplied (like nursery stock, chemicals, forestry capital equipment);
- those **outputs** which are exported, and which also have to be of consistent quality;
- and most **technological** aspects of the production process.

The developer may, however, choose to devolve some of this control to communities. Developers should also have strong influence, but not absolute control, over plantation purpose; staff management and training; infrastructure policy and management; species choice; forest management; harvesting; marketing; monitoring; and assuring ecosystem-wide (catchment) environmental benefits such as watershed management and conservation. Only rarely should the developer exercise abosolute control in one area.

Formal terms of partnership must spell out the system of compensation and incentives for communities. These might include profit-sharing and produce-sharing, provision of employment, purchase of local goods and services, subsidies, and the provision of community services. Technical management agreements may also be necessary as a regulatory framework.

In many tropical countries, outright purchase of land by the plantation developer is not feasible. It may also not be desirable for social reasons. Broadly speaking, other land-holding options can be divided into two categories: leases and joint venture arrangements. Both require the clear definition of land boundaries and land owners, and a legal system that allows a legal agreement to be registered against land title.

Within these two categories, there are further options. Where land is leased, the landowner may trade some of the rental for a share of forest products – this arrangement usually operates in favour of the plantation developer, for the landowner acquires a vested interest in maintaining productive plantations on his land. With joint ventures, the vested interest – and consequently the risk sharing – is greater; typically, the landowner contributes land and the developer contributes capital and technical management. In joint ventures, both partners should share management decisions – but in practice the landowner may voluntarily give up his management rights, for compensation. Landowners should still, however, be able to retain certain review and veto rights. In Fiji, joint venture plantation enterprises are being sold over completely, in stages, to the community (New Zealand Government 1989).

Established mechanisms are urgently needed for creating a balanced control of plantations between communities and industrial/corporate interests. In the long term, however, increased developer/community cooperation should help in the exploration of more appropriate roles. The social question promises to be perhaps the key issue for tropical plantations over the next few decades.

Endnote

This chapter was based in large part upon a paper prepared by one of us for the Shell International Petroleum Company and the World Wide Fund for Nature, UK (Bass 1992). We are grateful to Shell and WWF for permission to use this work, but stress that the opinions expressed are those of the authors and not necessarily those of Shell or WWF.

Box 5.1
Participatory and Rapid Rural Appraisal (P/RRA)

Participatory and Rapid Rural Appraisal (P/RRA) methods are frequently the most relevant and cost-effective for obtaining information about a community, the community's resources and its use of those resources. This is especially the case in remote areas, and in places which are poorly documented, such as are common in the tropics. P/RRA techniques allow appraisal staff to get information relatively quickly, at low cost, for purposes of planning activities within local economies and environments.

Various techniques exist, and they include more or less public participation (see McCracken et al. (1988) for a good overview). PRA, in particular, is designed for learning about a local situation from the perspective of local communities, and so is carried out entirely with local people.

Community profiles and diagrams illuminate key social, cultural, economic and ecological characteristics of the community; **calendars** of seasonal activity can reveal complementarities and constraints connected to the development of plantations alongside other land uses; **priority rankings** help community members to express current values, needs and opportunities; **local development and land-use histories** illustrate constraints and community attitudes towards forestry and land use; and **sketch maps** can point to appropriate plantation boundaries and the interactions of the proposed plantation with surrounding uses.

S.B

Box 5.2
Industrial plantations integrating local people's interests: the Paper Industry Corporation of the Philippines (PICOP)

PICOP is a Philippines corporation which runs a significant forest plantation enterprise, principally for supplying its large pulp mill. Most pulpwood plantations are under PICOP's own management, but it also supports local farmers as 'outgrowers'.

Under PICOP's outgrower scheme, local farmers with at least 5 ha within 100 km of PICOP's pulp mill are encouraged to grow trees for pulpwood. PICOP designed an agroforestry system to integrate *Eucalyptus deglupta* and *Albizia falcataria* cultivation with livestock and subsistence cropping – providing seedlings at cost, helping farmers with loans for 75 per cent of costs, and contracting to buy back the wood for a negotiated price. PICOP hired one extension worker for every 173 farmers, organized tree farmer associations, and broadcast advice daily on the radio.

PICOP chose municipal and *barrio* officials as its demonstration farmers. By 1981 there were 4,500 farms on 22,600 ha, supplying about a third of all the corporation's wood, although PICOP allows farmers to sell wood to other buyers if they can find a higher price. Technical assistance to farmers was based on PICOP's own plantation experience, but most farmers chose to adopt a low-labour method, covering land entirely with trees, rather than PICOP's more intensive agroforestry options.

The scheme has been profitable for both PICOP and smallholders. After the initial period, loans were necessary for encouraging only 30 per cent of the farmers to join the scheme. Labour accounts for most of the cost to the farmer, and so rates of return are very sensitive to changes in wages.

PICOP demonstrates a number of **principles of local involvement** in industrial plantations:

- participation open to all farmers with available land;
- providing good market information to farmers;
- assuring farmers of unequivocal rights to the trees and land in which farmers have invested;
- permitting multiple use of forested land;
- assuring the freedom to market produce anywhere;
- access to fair prices.

PICOP has had negative social experiences, too, however. Originally, the Manabos indigenous people and settlers in the area had problems keeping hold of their land and usufruct rights within the PICOP concession. Because the Marcos government saw PICOP as an important national asset, it sent military personnel to keep people out of the forests. This caused much local discontent, and specifically led to the area being a focal point for clashes between the government and the anti-Marcos New People's Army. In recent years, however, PICOP has granted land to indigenous people for subsistence farming and for small-scale tree plantations, and local people are employed as forest guards.

S.B.

Sources:
Bass, S., *Social and Cultural Issues*, Shell Tree Plantation Review Series, Study No. 4, London: Shell International and WWF, 1992.
Caufield, C., *In the Rainforest*, Heinemann, 1985.

Box 5.3
Gender issues in plantation feasibility studies

A plantation forestry assessment should consider whether gender issues are significant, and if so, how to accommodate gender-related differences in needs and aspirations.

In many cases women will form a major forest user group, motivated perhaps by the availability of subsistence resources such as firewood and fodder. The removal of access to such resources, e.g. when a natural forest is replaced by a plantation, must at least be adequately compensated for.

Ways should be sought for local women to participate in the appraisal and design of a prospective plantation. With representatives of women in the community, the feasibility study should determine:

- women's current involvement in forestry;
- women's potential involvement in forestry – especially to develop skills and earn income;
- the constraints to women realizing their potential in forestry: time, mobility, customs/taboos, land availability, ownership rights, information, training and education.

Except where this analysis clearly establishes that gender is not a major issue, the feasibility assessment should go on to obtain complete information concerning:

- the differential access of women to productive resources, employment and markets, especially in forestry and agriculture;
- particular forest products and services upon which women have a high dependency;
- particular forest products and services for the production of which women have a comparative advantage;
- the income differential of men and women;
- the differential ownership of assets, especially land and trees;
- women's workload and the division of work, especially with respect to forestry and agriculture;
- women's health and welfare conditions;
- women's education and training.

Mechanisms should then be designed to allow women to benefit from forest goods and services. Chambers *et al.* (1989) list possible mechanisms:

- strict enforcement of labour laws, particularly concerning minimum wages;
- in particularly segregated and hierarchical societies, special women's organizations and staff to increase confidence, representation and

   social acceptability;
- tenurial rights for women to be built in, even if social constraints and traditions require that they be introduced only gradually.

E.M./S.B.

CHAPTER 6

FOREST PLANTATIONS: TOWARDS SUSTAINABLE PRACTICE

Peter J. Kanowski and Peter S. Savill

Plantation forestry is, with a few notable exceptions, a relatively recent form of land use; most plantation forests have been established in the past fifty years. Nevertheless, a wealth of experience has accumulated over this period. Our purposes in this chapter are to describe the economic, environmental and social roles of plantation forestry; to synthesize relevant scientific and technical experience as a guide to best practice; and finally to suggest the research and development priorities to ensure that plantations will contribute to sustainable development in the future.

Plantation forests – what, where and why?

Plantation forestry has come to be synonymous with relatively high-input, intensive management of monocultures for the production of a relatively narrow range of products. In this sense, the development of forest plantation technology has paralleled that of agriculture generally. This approach will remain valid where land resources are not scarce and where the income from this form of plantation forestry exceeds that from alternative land uses. In many circumstances, particularly where land is scarce, time horizons short, or demand for non-wood products and services is strong, a broader range of plantation objectives and a more intimate integration with other land uses are likely to be necessary for successful plantation production. To some extent, this implies the need for redefining plantation forestry to promote an understanding of its potentially broader role. Thus, the simple and functional definition provided by Ford-Robinson (1971), of a 'forest crop or stand raised artificially', might be extended beyond the further classifications of Savill and Evans (1986) and Evans (1992):

> In its simplest form, plantation forestry describes the intensive management of a forest crop for a limited range of products. There

are circumstances in which this definition is appropriate, but many in which complex plantation forestry may be a better alternative. Complex plantation forestry also implies relatively intensive management which controls the origin, establishment and development of the forest crop, but which integrates other land uses within its boundaries, and which promotes the early and continuing production of a wide variety of goods, services and values.

Optimum management strategies for simple plantation forestry are generally well-defined, though not necessarily well-implemented. Those for complex plantation forestry, designed to maximize social benefits rather than wood production *per se*, are still being developed, and have much to gain from our experiences of a wide spectrum of forestry activities, including agroforestry, community forestry, and simple plantation forestry. This chapter summarizes what we have learnt from the practice of plantation forestry to date, and how we might adapt that knowledge to changing circumstances.

Extent, distribution, composition and production of plantation forests

Precise estimates of the extent of forest plantations are notoriously difficult to obtain, as definitions vary and the quality of some data is poor. The best current estimates (Mather 1990, Gauthier 1991, Sutton 1991, World Bank 1991) are of between 100 and 135 million hectares of plantations, about 75 per cent of which are temperate and 25 per cent in the tropics and subtropics. In total, plantations account for less that 3 per cent of global forest area. The regional distribution of the world's forests, including plantations, is summarized in Table 6.1. Global rates of plantation establishment and re-establishment are poorly known, but are estimated at around 1.2 million hectares annually in the tropics, and perhaps 10 million hectares in the temperate zones (Mather 1990).

The principal attraction of plantation forests is their productivity relative to most natural forest systems (Table 6.2). Most plantations have, therefore, been established primarily for industrial wood production, although Sutton (1991) estimates that only some 14 million hectares can be classified as 'fast-growing' (in his terms, where mean annual increment is greater than 14 m^3/hectare/year). The relatively small area of plantation forests belies their contribution to world wood supply, which has been increasing – in both absolute and relative terms throughout the twentieth century – as plantation stands reach maturity. Consequently,

Table 6.1 Forest and plantation areas by region (mid-1980s)

Region	Total forest and other wooded land (000 ha)	% of land area	Industrial plantations (000 ha); (% of world total)	Non-industrial plantations (000 ha) (% of world total)	Total plantations (000 ha); (% of world total)
Africa	1,339,077	45	1,925 [2]	2,484 [28]	4,409 [4]
Asia and Pacific	831,646	24	21,544 [22]	2,786 [32]	24,330 [23]
Central and S America	1,291,445	63	6,088 [6]	3,434 [40]	9,522 [9]
North America	734,476	40	11,950 [12]	...	11,950 [11][1]
Europe	178,353	38	25,159 [26]	...	25,159 [23][1]
Former USSR	929,600	42	21,900 [22]	...	21,900 [20]
World	5,304,597	40	98,566	8,704	107,270

Sources: Mather 1990, Gauthier 1991, Sutton 1991, World Bank 1991.
[1] These are probably under-estimates due to differences in classification.

plantations currently contribute 7–10 per cent of world industrial roundwood production (Gauthier 1991), projected to rise to up to half of total world wood supply by the year 2000 (Sedjo 1987). The vast majority of this wood will be best suited to pulp or other relatively low-value use (Sutton 1991) and, as Kallio *et al.* (1987) noted, the contribution of plantations in the developing world to international trade in forest products depends largely on trends in domestic consumption.

Species which have been most successfully cultivated in plantations are typically ecological pioneers, or those from early-successional stages, with light-demanding, colonizing characteristics: plantation conditions approximate their natural environment and tendency to grow in pure stands. Choice of species has been further constrained by the site types which have been available for afforestation, and the wood production objectives of most plantations. Therefore, species of only a few genera dominate existing plantation forests. *Eucalyptus* and *Pinus* are most common in warm temperate zones and in the tropics where, together with *Tectona grandis*, they account for about 85 per cent of plantation area. Cool temperate plantations are dominated by species of *Picea* and *Pinus*, with other taxa such as *Larix* and *Populus*, or *Pseudotsuga menziesii*, of regional importance. Where objectives other than industrial wood production predominate, so do other genera such as *Acacia* or *Leucaena*. Few tropical hardwood species of commercial value appear to have the ecological characteristics appropriate to simple plantation forestry under current practice, and it is principally for this reason that attempts at their culture in plantation have rarely been successful.

Rationales for plantations

The industrial wood production objective of the majority of the world's plantation forests (Table 6.1) derives from a complex array of forces. Principal amongst these has been the perceived role of forest resources in economic development – first enunciated by Westoby (1962), and subsequently reviewed by, amongst others, Douglas (1983), Westoby himself (1987), Byron and Waugh (1988) and Binkley and Vincent (1992). The rationale for the establishment of plantation forests for both industrial and non-industrial purposes is closely linked to economic development:

1. As a resource base for the development of **wood-using industries**. Plantations may represent a new resource (e.g. Portugal, Swaziland) or a replacement for diminishing (e.g. Malaysia, United Kingdom) or

Table 6.2 Productivity (annual wood increment) of various well-managed
forest types

Forest type	Mean annual increment $(m^3/ha/year)$
Tropics and sub-tropics	
Natural forests	
Deciduous woodland (range)[1]	1–2
Rainforest (extensive management)[2]	1.5–15
Plantation forests	
Lowland hardwoods (range)[2]	10–20
Lowland eucalypts and conifers (range)[2]	20–35
Montane eucalypts and conifers (range)[1]	30–40
Aracruz, Brazil: *Eucalyptus* hybrids[3]	50
Temperate regions	
Natural forests	
Canada: conifers (average)[4]	1.0
USA: conifers (average)[4]	2.6
Sweden: conifers (average)[4]	3.3
Australia: southern eucalypts (average)[5]	7.3
Plantation forests	
UK: broadleaves (average)[4]	5.0
UK: conifers (average)[4]	11.0
Portugal: *Eucalyptus globulus* (range)[6]	3–40
Portugal: *Eucalyptus globulus* (average)[7]	13
New Zealand: *Pinus radiata*[3]	18–30

Sources: [1] Dawkins 1992; [2] Dawkins 1967; [3] Sturm 1991; [4] Savill and Evans 1986; [5] Risby 1987; [6] Pereira and Santos Pereira 1988; [7] Cotterill 1992.

less productive (e.g. Australia, Brazil) natural forests. The economic rationale may be one of import substitution (e.g. Australia, United Kingdom, Zimbabwe) or generation of export income (e.g. Chile, New Zealand, Venezuela).

2. As an **energy source**, for either industrial (e.g. wood gas, ethanol) or

non-industrial (e.g. fuelwood, charcoal) production (Davidson 1987), particularly in areas where fuelwood deficits are severe (e.g. the Indian sub-continent, the Sahel region).

3. For provision of **rural employment** in circumstances where labour is available and its cost is relatively low. In economically developed countries, the historically high levels of employment required for plantation establishment and management have been supplanted by mechanization (e.g. Stewart 1987). However, in economies where labour costs are relatively low, plantation programmes continue to have considerable potential to generate employment (Davidson 1987).

4. Maintenance or enhancement of **agricultural productivity** (e.g. Rosenberg 1974, Felker 1981).

In other cases, environmental concerns have prompted plantation establishment for:

5. **Environmental protection or rehabilitation**, especially soil and slope stablilization (e.g. Egypt, Saudi Arabia, China, Japan, Nepal, Switzerland).

6. **Protection of natural forests** from exploitation for either commercial use (e.g. Australia; Cameron and Penna 1988) or subsistence needs (e.g. Bangladesh; Davidson 1987) – although the effect has often been the opposite (see Chapter 2).

7. **Carbon sequestration**, in an attempt to mitigate global warming (e.g. Grainger 1991).

Governments have, therefore, often sought to promote plantation forestry, for one or more of the reasons above. They have done so directly, by financing plantation afforestation programmes through, variously, state forestry agencies (e.g. Australia, China, Kenya, New Zealand) or parastatal companies (e.g. Fiji, India, Malaysia), and indirectly, through grants, subsidies or tax concessions (e.g. Brazil, Chile, United Kingdom). Where large private investors are involved in plantation forestry, they are likely to be motivated by the expectation of:

8. Attractive **financial returns**, over the long term, relative to other investments.

Although plantations have usually been developed on land which is owned or managed by the state or large-scale forest industries, smaller private landholders have been regionally important (e.g. Philippines, New

Zealand; McGaughey and Gregersen 1988), and are likely to become more so in the future as pressures for land increase (see Box 5.2). There is a wealth of information describing the characteristics and motivation of these forest growers in both industrial and non-industrial societies (e.g. Arnold 1983, Blatner and Greene 1989, FAO 1985a, McGaughey and Gregersen 1988). Their rationales for plantation establishment may reflect, to varying degrees, elements of those outlined above. They may also include:

9. **Productive use of land which has become surplus** as a consequence of altered farming systems or reduced labour availability (e.g. Kenya - Dewees 1991, Europe - Hummel 1991). In some cases, plantation establishment may reinforce individuals' **land tenure rights** (e.g. Ecuador – Gondard 1988).
10. **Income-generation** opportunities in response to local market shortages, however transitory (e.g. India – Saxena 1991).
11. **Investment strategies** which emphasize capital accumulation in the tree crop, rather than income generation (Arnold 1983, Chambers and Leach 1989).

In reality, these rationales often interact, and any individual plantation is likely to be established as the result of a variety of these forces.

Decisions about how forests and trees are used are largely defined by proclaimed or *de facto* policies which govern land use, land tenure, forestry activities, and forest industries and markets, and by policies bearing on these activities which transform forests to other uses. The circumstances most favourable to the successful development of forest plantations are those in which a coordinated land-use strategy has been formulated and agreed, tenure rights are unambiguous and unchallenged, forestry is treated as more than a residual land use, the relative roles of natural and plantation forests are well-defined, and forest industries or markets are sufficiently developed and stable enough to maintain a relatively assured demand for forest products. The financial and biological characteristics of trees as plantation crops also have important conse-quences for decisions concerning plantation forestry.

Trees as plantation crops

The primary distinguishing feature of trees as plantation crops is their relatively long production period, seldom less than four years, commonly of ten or more years, traditionally at least twenty-five years in the tropics, and commonly at least twice that in temperate regions. Successful plantation programmes, whether on a large or small scale, therefore require the commitment of adequate resources over a considerable time period, and depend on security of land tenure, assured rights to the tree crop, strong and continuing technical input at the appropriate level, and linkage to markets.

Financial characteristics and consequences

In the case of most simple forest plantation crops grown primarily for wood production, costs – planning, acquisition and raising of planting stock, site evaluation and preparation, planting and maintenance – are concentrated in the early phases, and returns from harvesting in the late stages, of the production period. As financial evaluations based on present value criteria are strongly influenced by the time between investment and return, this period – approximated for most plantation species by their rotation length – is critical in determining the financial returns from tree growing. The major consequence is that private investment in plantation forestry can probably only be expected in economies which are perceived to be stable over the period of investment (Yoho 1985), and for species and sites from which favourable financial returns are most assured.

Governments have, therefore, often had a leading role in undertaking or facilitating plantation afforestation (Hurditch 1992). However, financial returns from plantation forestry are not necessarily poor: McGaughey and Gregersen (1988) suggested that the return on investment for well-managed, fast growing, industrial-tree crops should be in the order of 10–15 per cent, consistent with the 8–12 per cent internal rates of return reported by Elliott et al. (1989) and Whiteside (1989) for New Zealand Eucalyptus and Pinus radiata plantations. At the higher end of this range, returns on investment are comparable to those from rubber plantations (Young 1990). Although returns from slower-growing plantations are probably more in the order of 2–5 per cent (e.g. Wilson 1989, Spilsbury 1990), they nevertheless compare favourably to real rates of return from other long-term investments (Leslie 1989). The returns from any particular plantation programme will depend on a myriad of biological factors (e.g. growth rate) and economic factors (e.g. capital and labour costs), and on the consequent environmental and social costs and benefits.

Although the issue of public or private ownership has been hotly debated in many countries (e.g. New Zealand – Kirkland 1989; United Kingdom – Rickman 1991), this is more a matter of politics than economics. The successful involvement of both large and small-scale private investors in plantation forestry in many countries (e.g. Chile – Hurditch 1992; India – Srivastavea *et al.* 1986, *Indian Forester* 1991; New Zealand – Elliott *et al.* 1989) suggests that factors other than the economic characteristics of trees themselves are the primary determinants of the level and source of investment. A secure investment environment and sufficient investment capital are probably most critical. Depending on the scale of private firms' or individuals' holdings, it is taxation arrangements which do not discriminate against forestry, or the availability of credit on appropriate terms for tree growing, which may be most important in facilitating private plantation forestry (Arnold 1983, McGaughey and Gregersen 1988, Brunton 1987).

The foregoing discussion assumes that investment decisions are made primarily on the basis of discounted net benefit, which is likely to apply to many large investors. There is considerable debate over the more general relevance and application of this criterion (e.g. Leslie 1987, 1989; Price, in press); in any case, for many small-scale growers, the risks and cash flows associated with plantation forestry are more likely to determine their behaviour than are evaluations based on net income over a long time period. Schemes by which industrial wood users enter into agreements with private landholders for the supply of wood are often successful (e.g. Philippines – see Box 5.2; Portugal – Borralho, 1992), and may involve the purchaser in establishment and management of the plantations. In such cases, there is usually the added advantage of more efficient and more satisfactory operations, in both environmental and social terms.

Biological characteristics and consequences

In circumstances where complex plantation forestry is appropriate, the biological characteristics of trees may be more important in determining plantation success than are financial characteristics. Species and management regimes which do not integrate well with other land uses may be inappropriate. In some cases, the adoption of complex plantation forestry may require only a modification of traditional silvicultural principles (e.g. Gilmour *et al.* 1990). In others, a synthesis of agroforestry and plantation forestry approaches will be desirable (e.g. Sargent 1990). Elsewhere, replacement of species which produce only wood by those which also yield valuable intermediate returns may offer the best solution (e.g. Keresztesi 1983). Depending on the tree species and silvicultural regime, a variety of agroforestry practices, e.g. intercropping, underplanting, or rotational cropping, may be feasible, according to particular circumstances and demands. The relative merits of each will depend on the biological and economic characteristics and interactions of the tree and non-tree crops, the sustainable land-use systems with which local people are familiar or which can be introduced, and the risks and cash flows associated with each option. The use of 'multi-purpose' species may be dependent upon developments in technology to facilitate multiple uses: for example, progress in the processing and marketing of rubberwood (*Hevea brasiliensis*) allows it to be considered as an alternative to more conventional forest plantation crops such as *Acacia mangium* (Malaysian Timber Industry Board 1988).

Implementing plantation forestry

Plantation forestry should be implemented according to a definition of sustainability sufficiently broad to encompass its biological, economic and social dimensions (e.g. Ascher and Healy 1990, Barbier 1987). Although there are many difficulties in the definition and evaluation of sustainability (e.g. Caldwell 1990, Cocklin 1989), the concept creates a framework within which acceptable plantation practice can be defined.

Within this framework, effective planning and management are critical to the success of any plantation programme. Both involve iterative processes of defining objectives, formulating alternative means of attaining them, estimating their impacts and assessing their costs and benefits, revising proposals as necessary, and selecting, implementing, monitoring and redefining, as necessary, the best option(s). In the sections that follow, we discuss the coordinated sequence of activities necessary for sustainable plantation forestry.

Planning, impact assessment and monitoring

A principal requirement is accurate information describing the land resource and its biophysical characteristics, current users and use patterns, and relevant social and economic issues. The form in which this information is presented is important; it must be accessible to the range of interested parties (Davis-Case 1989). Much of the geographic and biophysical data can be usefully presented as maps, at a scale of 1:10 000 or less; the development of geographic information systems has greatly facilitated their processing and presentation. The form in which other information is presented will depend on its nature and intended audience (e.g. Chambers *et al.* 1989).

These data should form the basis for draft proposals for review by appropriate state agencies and, at least, those individuals or groups directly affected by, or with a recognized interest in, the planned development. A planning process which invites comment at this stage, and is seen to respond to it, is more likely to gain eventual acceptance than one which does not. Numerous ideotypes and procedures (e.g. Blair and Olpadwala 1988, Cassells and Valentine 1988, Davies-Case 1989, Knopp and Caldbeck 1990) have been suggested or implemented to address this challenge, which is discussed in more detail in Chapter 5.

Plantation planning

Successful plantation establishment and sustainable management demands integrated planning at all levels. Minimum planning requirements for plantation forests are (adapted from ITTO 1991):

1. Clear definition of objectives. It is only after these have been specified that appropriate sites, species and technologies can be proposed and evaluated.
2. Recognition of customary rights and local demands, and their consequences for forest composition, design and management.
3. Prior survey to identify and protect areas of conservation and cultural significance, physical fragility, landscape value and hydrology. These areas should be reserved from afforestation and protected from damage.
4. Plantation design to retain a network of natural vegetation and avoid intrusion of watercourses (e.g. Queensland Department of Forestry 1987, Sargent 1990). The location and construction of access and extraction roading and of fire protection networks is particularly important in this context.
5. Definition of site preparation, establishment, management and harvesting regimes which minimize adverse environmental impacts (e.g. Forestry Commission of Tasmania 1989, Queensland Department of Forestry 1987).
6. Definition of plans for protection against and management of fire, biological pests and diseases (e.g. Manion 1991, Speight and Wainhouse 1989).
7. Derivation of product utilization and marketing strategies (e.g. Barbour and Kellogg 1990, McGaughey and Gregersen 1988).

Assessment of impacts

Plantations are established within a physical matrix which may be loosely termed the 'site', which is a complex of physical, chemical, biotic and social/cultural factors. Physical factors include the soils in which plantations are established, and the topography and elevation of the landscape; chemical factors include soil fertility and atmospheric pollution; biotic factors include the plant and animal communities which the plantation might influence, or which might affect the growth of the trees; and social/cultural factors concern the human communities around which the plantation is established and which interact with it.

Whatever the objectives and management strategy adopted, the maintenance of environmental quality and integration into local societies and land-use practices are minimum requirements for plantation forests. Environmental impacts are typically identified and evaluated through preparation of an *Environmental Impact Statement* (Hyman and Siftel 1988), and usually addressed by the definition of operating standards and codes of practice (e.g. Forestry Commission of Tasmania 1989, ITTO 1990 and 1991, Poore and Sayer 1987). Establishing the plantation programme in the broader social context is somewhat more challenging, although appraisal and diagnosis methodologies (e.g. Formby 1986, Anon 1987, Raintree 1987, Molnar 1989) have been developed to offer some guidance. (See Chapter 5.)

Auditing and monitoring

Environmental auditing and a long-term monitoring system are necessary to describe plantation impacts objectively, preferably quantitatively, and to assess the sustainability of plantation crops over successive rotations. In addition, an objective means of monitoring provides a way not only of detecting long-term changes, but it also has many short-term managerial uses, such as the preparation of yield models and estimating future production. It can also provide a means of detecting nutrient deficiencies, pest outbreaks and other problems which might be unknown at the time of establishment.

Monitoring systems usually take the form of a network of permanent sample plots (normally of 0.01 or 0.02 hectares), stratified by species, soil type, age class and region. They need not be very numerous – say one plot per 20 to 50 hectares – and can, if necessary, be supplemented by temporary plots for specific purposes (e.g. Adlard 1990; Alder and Synott 1992). An important feature is that they should be **permanent**, that is they should be carried on from one rotation to the next on exactly the same spot. Sample plots should be measured at intervals which depend to some extent on the climate and site. Those in relatively slow-growing temperate forests might be remeasured at five to ten year intervals, as well as at the time of thinning, while in the humid tropics, where growth and impacts are more rapid, measurements should be more frequent.

The design and conduct of auditing and monitoring systems have been described elsewhere (e.g. Shell 1989). Whilst initiation of a monitoring programme is usually the task of a specialist, its maintenance is neither expensive nor difficult. It is essential that field managers appreciate the reasons for its existence and its potential value, and are therefore motivated to maintain it.

Plantation technology, genetics and management

Contemporary forest management has a certain dualism. One element is the sophisticated, quantitative management science which has been developed for large-scale simple plantation forestry. Planning and analysis methodologies are usually based on mathematical optimization, and have been developed for purposes such as multiple-use planning, harvest scheduling, and evaluating silvicultural alternatives. Approaches and systems are well described by, e.g., Clutter *et al.* (1983), Dykstra (1984), Hoekstra *et al.* (1987), Leuschner (1984), and Whyte (1989). However, the simplifications inherent in mathematical modelling also limit many of these approaches, which have been criticized for their emphasis on wood production (e.g. Behan 1990, Maser 1990).

In parallel, there has been increasing acknowledgement of the value of traditional management systems as similarly sophisticated, albeit in a qualitative manner, and the development of new management practices which build upon them. The progressive understanding of these systems and their interactions with societies are recorded in the development literature (e.g. Arnold and Stewart 1991, Arnold 1991, Cook and Grut 1989, FAO 1985a, Leach and Mearns 1988). This evolving understanding has much to contribute to the development of complex plantation forestry.

In the sections that follow, we review briefly the major technical elements of plantation forestry. These technical elements apply regardless of the simplicity or complexity of the plantation forestry activities, and comprise:

• choice and improvement of genetic resources;
• production of planting stock;

- site preparation;
- establishment;
- tending;
- spacing, thinning and pruning;
- harvesting and regeneration.

The implementation of these activities follows from, and takes place in the context of, the planning, assessment and monitoring process described above (see p.130–3). Although each can be represented, discussed and implemented independently, it is their integration into a coordinated system which will make plantation forestry successful. Foresters are continually having to choose between different silvicultural and management systems to achieve different mixes of products and benefits from specific forest areas in particular circumstances: there is no single system ideal for all situations. Where the necessary resources and management expertise are available, the productive capacity of plantations is unlikely to be rivalled; where such interventions are less certain, so should the expectations of and reliance on plantations diminish.

Choice and improvement of genetic resources

Appropriate genetic resources provide the biological foundation of successful plantation forestry. The consequences of sub-optimum genetic material are, at worst, plantation failure or, at best, reduced plantation health, productivity, quality and economic viability (e.g. Evans 1992, Gibson et al. 1983, Hughes 1989, Camphinos and Ikemori 1989, Kanowski and Nikles 1989, Moran and Bell 1987, Zobel et al. 1987).

Genetic resources of plantation species The term 'genetic resources' describes the gene pool of both wild and cultivated populations of a species. Populations of cultivated tree species have high levels of genetic diversity relative to other plants (National Research Council 1991), a consequence of both their biological characteristics and generally short history of domestication. The genetic resources of currently or potentially important plantation species are widely distributed: many are represented primarily in natural populations, and are threatened by forest loss or degradation (e.g. National Research Council 1991, Sayer and Whitmore 1991). The success of efforts to conserve these genetic resources *in situ*, largely through reservation, has been variable.

Genetic resources may also be conserved *ex situ*, in the form of seeds and plants or stands managed explicitly for the purposes of genetic conservation. Existing plantation forests also represent a genetic resource, although sometimes one of limited value because of a narrow genetic base (e.g. *Eucalyptus globulus* in Portugal – Pereira and Santos Pereira 1988; *Pinus radiata* in Australasia – Moran and Bell 1987). There have been major efforts over the past thirty years, coordinated or led by a variety of international and national agencies, to conserve the genetic resources of many species (National Research Council 1991; *Forest Ecology and Management* 1990). However, the National Research Council (1991) concluded that 'no adequate global strategy exists for systematically identifying, sampling, testing, and breeding trees with potential use'; it suggested that 'efforts to conserve and manage tree genetic resources do not encompass global needs', and recommended a tenfold increase in the number of species included in genetic conservation programmes. One of the objectives of the current expansion of the Consultative Group on International Agricultural Research (CGIAR) system to encompass tree species is to address such needs.

The current availability of genetic resources varies greatly, therefore, with species. Typically, the international agencies with a genetic conservation role cooperate with local institutions in the collection and distribution of small quantities of seed for research purposes, and in the establishment and assessment of genetic trials. The National Research Council (1991) lists these agencies. A policy of open access has prevailed for the genetic resources of most species, although the issue, and that of plant variety rights, are the subject of increasing debate (e.g. Marshall 1989, 1990). The recent Costa Rican example of substantial commercial (pharmaceutical company) funding for the integrated exploration and conservation of forest genetic resources may offer a stimulus to similar efforts elsewhere.

Acquisition of adequate genetic resources for larger-scale afforestation is often more problematic. Tree seed is widely traded and, although information and controls concerning its origin and genetic quality have improved (e.g. Midgley 1988), uncertainties remain in many cases. The agencies responsible for seed collection for research purposes (see National Research Council 1991) can usually provide information about reliable and reputable suppliers of commercial quantities of seed for plantation programmes. The advanced breeding programmes developed for many species, by both public agencies and private enterprises, are usually able to supply large quantities of genetically improved seed or propagules, which should be tested on a pilot scale along with accessions from natural populations.

Selection and testing of genetic resources The genetic resources appropriate for particular plantations will depend on:

1. The **purposes** for which afforestation takes place. There is enormous genetic variation in most characteristics between and within most species. In the case of simple plantation forestry, wood production and quality traits are likely to be of greatest interest; in the case of more complex plantation forestry, a range of traits such as the interaction of the species with crops, the palatability and nutritional value of its foliage, fruiting characteristics, the calorific value of its wood, or its ability to coppice from stump, may be of greater significance (e.g. Boland 1989).
2. The **environmental characteristics** of the sites available for establishment. Typically, sites available for plantation establishment have been those not favoured for agriculture or degraded by over-exploitation. For example, salt-affected lands, of which there are some 150 million hectares in the tropics, have potential for afforestation if suitable species and genetic stock is made available. Soil physical and nutritional characteristics have therefore been poor, and sites may also be more subject to climatic extremes. Consequently, the range of species which can be successfully established may be limited, at least initially. In such cases, simple plantation forestry may be a necessary precursor to the development of more complex ecosystems (e.g. Gilmour *et al.* 1990).
3. The level of **information** about and **availability** of genetic resources. Where only limited samples of a species' genetic resources are available for testing, trial results should be interpreted with due caution, as they may not be representative of the species' potential. The widespread use of material of limited genetic base also risks exposure to pests or disease (e.g. *Leucaena leucocephala* in Asia; Hughes 1989), although some species so far appear resilient despite the narrow genetic base of most exotic plantings (e.g. *Grevillea robusta* worldwide; Harwood 1989).
4. The **technical skills** of those responsible for afforestation, and the human and financial resources available for programme implementation. Successful establishment and maintenance of some species (e.g. many eucalypts) on some sites requires intensive site preparation, control of competing vegetation, and relatively intensive management. Other species (e.g. some acacias) are much less demanding of management intervention.

The basis of species and provenance (the geographic origin of the seed) selection is the matching of their requirements to site characteristics, so as to avoid stress to the crop. In principle, it is preferable to use local provenances of native species, adapted to local soil, climatic and biotic conditions. However, whilst there are many examples of successful plantation forestry with native species – *Quercus* in Europe (Savill and Kanowski 1991), *Pinus* in North America (Duryea and Dougherty 1990), or *Araucaria* in Australia (Queensland Department of Forestry 1987), there are many environments in which exotic species or provenances have proved superior – in terms of productivity and/or quality – to local sources (e.g. Evans 1992, Zobel *et al.* 1987). The reasons for the superiority of exotics vary with species and environment, ranging from an absence of specialized pathogens and predators to greater tolerance of degraded sites (Evans 1992, Savill and Evans 1986, Zobel *et al.* 1987). Although recent advances in bioclimatic analyses (e.g. Booth *et al.* 1989) have facilitated the selection of species and provenances likely to succeed in particular environments, there remains no substitute for extensive and extended testing of potential introductions in field trials and the dissemination of data from them (e.g. Brown *et al.* 1989).

Genetic improvement of plantation species Genetic improvement of pure or hybrid species is a feature common to most successful plantation programmes. It is helpful to conceptualize forest genetic and tree improvement activities in terms of the three phases identified by Cheliak and Rogers (1990):

1. **Conservation**. In addition to efforts at genetic resource conservation *per se*, as discussed above, it is also possible and desirable to design breeding strategies which specify the maintenance of genetic diversity as an explicit objective (e.g. Burdon 1989a, Kang and Nienstaedt 1987, Kitzmiller 1990, Namkoong *et al.* 1980, 1988).
2. **Selection, breeding and testing**, based on the recurrent cycle described by White (1987). Cotterill (1986) demonstrated that, in most cases, relatively simple methods can be as effective as more complex alternatives.
3. **Propagation**, i.e. the transfer of gains realized by genetic improvement from the breeding population to operational production. Currently feasible propagation options are the production of genetically-improved seed or the vegetative multiplication of outstanding genotypes; the former is generally cheaper, and the latter generally quicker. The additional cost of vegetatively propagated plants increases with the difficulty of propagation, and is typically a minimum of 30–50 per cent more than that of seedlings (Savill and Evans 1986). Consequently, Burdon (1989b) suggested that clonal forestry on an

operational scale may be worthwhile only for those taxa which are easily propagated.

The means by which each of these activities is achieved and coordinated is the breeding strategy. A variety of simple and relatively cheap breeding strategies are available (e.g. Barnes and Mullin 1989, Kanowski and Savill 1991, Namkoong 1989) and adaptable to the many circumstances of plantation forestry. There is sufficient genetic variation in and control of most traits to allow productivity gains in the order of 30–50 per cent from the first generation of breeding (e.g. Kanowski *et al.* 1989). Programmes based on short rotation species have demonstrated that substantial gains can be maintained over at least several generations (e.g. Franklin 1989). The cost of genetically-improved material is a trivial proportion, typically not more than a few per cent (e.g. Cameron and Lieshout 1988), of plantation establishment costs. Where economic analyses have been conducted, they suggest that investment in tree improvement as part of a plantation programme is well justified, especially where rotations are relatively short (e.g. Borralho *et al.* in press, Cameron and Lieshout 1988, Evans 1992, Whiteside 1989, Zobel and Talbert 1984).

The integration of developments in biotechnology into tree-breeding programmes offers further opportunities for more accelerated and targeted genetic improvement (Cheliak and Rogers 1990). However, the use of these new, sophisticated and expensive technologies should be seen as complementing, rather than substituting for, traditional selective breeding, which is cheap and robust by comparison, and from which much genetic gain can be realized. While the application of biotechnologies to tree species will doubtless increase rapidly, the generally low unit value of most tree crops suggests that, as Cheliak and Rogers (1990) noted:

its development should be viewed as a means to enhance our abilities to solve specific problems . . . successful application of biotechnology is conditional on an established and aggressive conventional [tree improvement] program. Without this, biotechnology makes little sense.

Production of planting stock

Plantations can be established by direct sowing of seed, with seedlings raised in nurseries, or with clonal propagules originating from cuttings or tissue culture. Establishment with seedlings is typical, but the use of clonal plantlets is increasing rapidly, particularly in short-rotation forestry (Burdon 1989b). Information describing seed collection, handling, processing, storage, testing and germination requirements is usually essential in either case, and is well documented for many species (e.g. FAO 1985b). Appropriate propagation techniques have been developed for many plantation species, and are under development for many others (Barnes and Burley 1987, Burdon 1989b, Purse 1989).

Successful production of either seedlings or clonal propagules demands good nursery practice, the elements of which are well developed and documented (e.g. Aldhous 1984, ILO 1990, Queensland Department of Forestry 1987). The desirable attributes in the quality of nursery stock are well understood, and have been described in detail by Evans (1992) for the tropics, and by Savill and Evans (1986) for temperate regions.

The successful transfer, in terms of survival and subsequent growth, of nursery stock to the field is greatly enhanced by using the appropriate type of plant for the site, demanding effective quality control in the nursery. Containerized plants are more expensive than bare-rooted stock, but their use extends the planting season, and allows species not amenable to bare-root establishment to be planted.

Given good nursery stock, adequate site preparation, proper planting and satisfactory early maintenance, plantation establishment rates (i.e. tree survival rates) should average at least 85 per cent. Many early plantation failures are attributable to poor nursery technique, inexcusable given the wealth of readily-available knowledge about appropriate methodologies. There is no universally favoured or correct technique of either nursery production or planting: the choice depends on species, site and the availability of labour, equipment and finance.

Site assessment and preparation

Most sites available for plantation establishment require some preparation prior to planting, to optimize tree survival and subsequent growth (e.g. Duryea and Dougherty 1990, Evans 1992). Appropriate site preparation measures vary from drainage of potentially waterlogged sites, as in much of upland Britain, to ensuring that as much moisture as possible is retained on site, as in the terracing practised in many Mediterranean countries. Cultivation prior to planting has numerous advantages: the disruption or loosening of compacted layers, such as iron pans in the soil, allowing deep rooting and better water retention; the incorporation of surface organic matter; and the control of potentially competing woody or herbaceous vegetation. Appropriate site preparation probably has a more pronounced impact on stand nutrition than any other silvicultural practice, including fertilization.

Definition of the appropriate preparation system for a site requires analysis of:

1. **Climate**. For example, rainfall distribution patterns and fire hazard will determine the timing and objective of preparation, and the permissibility of retaining substantial quantities of woody material on site.
2. **Species characteristics and requirements**. Tolerance of impeded drainage, root penetration and competition, for example, varies with species; the level of site preparation necessary will similarly vary.
3. **Site parameters**. Soil characteristics and site factors – topography, slope, and aspect – are major determinants of cultivation methods. In general, the better the soil and site conditions, the lower the risks of degradation and permanent site damage. It is usually impossible to ameliorate soils of poor texture, such as silts or heavy clays, but easier to improve inadequate chemical or nutritional status. Steep slopes and fragile soils are at most risk from erosion or damage, and should only be included in plantations if they can be prepared, established and harvested without adverse impact.
4. **Cultivation options**. Mechanical site preparation is widely used, but not necessarily always required or preferable; more labour-intensive methods may be more appropriate in some circumstances. In all cases, it is important to minimize the duration of soil exposure, both to prevent erosion and to retain nutrients on the site. Heavy machinery can also cause serious compaction of some soils, which can have adverse consequences on tree crops. Removing topsoil or organic matter can reduce the site's nutrient capital, nutrient availability, and potential for productivity (Duryea and Dougherty 1990).
5. **Soil conservation status**. Appropriate soil conservation measures should be seen as an integral part of the site preparation system; they will depend on the climatic and site characteristics and the cultivation options outlined above.

(Foster and Constantini 1991)

Plantation establishment

Appropriate methods for establishing trees (i.e. getting them in the ground and growing well) have been well described and documented for many environments (e.g. Chapman and Allan 1978, Evans 1992, Hibberd

1991). A variety of manual and semi-mechanized techniques are available; their applicability depends on site type, plant type, and relative costs. Correct timing is essential: for example, in climates where the rainfall is seasonal, it is normal to plant at the time when the rainy season has reliably started; where cold winters occur, planting is often during the dormant season, or just at the end of it.

The replacement of dead plants after establishment, usually within a year of the initial planting, is commonly done but is often wasteful, as the growth of replacements usually fall far behind that of the original plants. Replacement is usually only worthwhile if failures are very numerous, or if gaps are larger than the space occupied by one final crop tree (about $25m^2$). If it is necessary, then the plants used should be especially large and vigorous so that they are able to compete with the original trees. It is far preferable to try to ensure that the original planting is completely successful.

Protection of trees from animal damage and fire is usually most critical in the early post-establishment phase. Where populations of browsing animals are high, some form of fencing is usually necessary to protect young plants (Chapman and Allan 1978, Evans 1992, Savill and Evans 1986). Fire protection is discussed below.

Tending

The operations known as 'tending' include all those between establishment and first thinning. Many species require timely silvicultural interventions if they are to attain their potential. This in turn means sustained financing, delegation of authority to field officers, and an efficient short-linked command structure. It is always more cost-effective to ensure that what is already planted becomes properly established than to plant more. Growth quality which has been lost due to poor management or maintenance can never be regained, and results in longer rotations and reduced product quality and value. The major components of tending – vegetation management, nutrition, and pest and disease management – are outlined below.

Vegetation management The growth and development of the plantation crop is retarded when other vegetation competes with it for light, water and nutrients. Competing plants are defined as weeds. Weed competition is most intense during the period from establishment until the tree canopy has closed, after which the shade cast by the canopy generally suppresses weed growth and competition.

Weed control in the first few years of plantation development is, therefore, often critical to the survival and satisfactory growth of the tree crop. Some common plantation species, such as poplars and eucalypts, are so sensitive to competition that, unless weed control is very thorough, extensive plantation failure can be expected. Even for less sensitive species, adequate weed control results in dramatic improvements to growth, often in the order of 50 to 100 per cent (Wilkinson and Neilsen 1990, Queensland Department of Forestry 1989).

However, 'weed' species can have important funtions in plantation ecosystems. They form part of a semi-natural community of organisms, protecting the soil structure and surface, providing habitats for predators of organisms which damage crop plants, acting as a temporary reservoir for nutrients in young crops – nutrients which may otherwise be lost from the site, and providing a source of food for browsing animals. In their absence, these animals would often damage the tree crop. Appropriate management of competing vegetation is, therefore, seldom aimed at eliminating all weeds on the site, but is more directed and considered.

Appropriate vegetation management systems aim to define, create and maintain a weed-free growth zone around each tree. They are cheaper, more cost-effective, and more environmentally desirable than approaches involving total control. Under a managed approach, weeds are controlled only to the extent that they limit the crop's development. The size of the growth zone to be maintained in a weed-free condition varies with species and age of the crop. The radius of the optimum weed-free zone in tropical and sub-tropical eastern Australia increases from 0.9 m, in the first year after establishment, to 1.5 m subsequently (Queensland Department of Forestry 1989). In less weed-prone environments, use of 1 m wide bands straddling each line of trees, or circles of 0.5 m radius around each tree, is common and generally adequate. These zones can be maintained by manual, motor-manual, mechanical or chemical means (Evans 1992).

A variety of other vegetation management methodologies are also available, and should be used where possible; many are particularly suited to complex plantation forestry. They include stand manipulation to make use of the competitive abilities of the trees themselves e.g. traditional French oak silviculture (Benezit 1991); the use of particular cover crops e.g. pasture legumes (Boardman 1988); multiple cropping and taungya systems (Evans 1992); biological control e.g. of *Lantana camara* (Evans 1992); and the controlled use of fire, which is only possible when the tree crop is of sufficient size to withstand low-intensity burning.

Nutrition The nutritional demands which a plantation crop makes of the soil depend primarily on its stage of development (Attiwell 1979, Miller

1981). The period from establishment to canopy closure, typically between two and ten years in most plantations, is known as the canopy-building phase. During this period relatively large amounts of nutrients are required, and growth is likely to suffer if any of some fifteen essential nutrient elements is deficient or inaccessible in the soil. Many sites available for plantation establishment are grossly deficient in phosphorus or nitrogen (e.g. Dickson and Savill 1974), or lacking essential micronutrients such as boron, zinc or copper (Binns *et al.* 1980, Whyte 1988). In these cases, fertilizer application is essential for successful plantation development. In addition, the presence of particular symbiotic micro-organisms, e.g. *Rhizobium* in the case of some legumes, or *Frankia* in the case of *Casuarina* and *Alnus* species, is necessary for these species to fix atmospheric nitrogen. Most trees also have mycorrhizal fungi associated with their roots, with a critical role in nutrient uptake. The absence of any of these micro-organisms can severely retard growth, and it may be necessary to introduce them to plantation soils, particularly when exotic species are first introduced.

Recycling of nutrients, rather than their acquisition from mineral soil reserves, becomes the dominant process after canopy closure, once the nutrient capital of the stand has been accumulated, primarily within the foliage. The fall of leaves and other litter, their subsequent decomposition and release of nutrients, substantially reduces the dependence of the trees on soil nutrient reserves. These recycled nutrients, together with enhanced inputs from the capture by tree canopies of atmospheric nutrients in rainfall, gases and aerosols, generally meet the stand's requirements. The common exception is nitrogen, which can become immobilized when deep litter layers develop as the stand ages.

The nutritional status of a plantation is therefore a consequence not just of soil and parent material, but also of management practices (e.g. Boardman 1988). The treatment of organic material including woody debris (e.g. whether it is cultivated into the soil or burnt), the use of leguminous cover crops, or the interaction with weeds, can have major effects on nutrient availability (e.g. Boardman 1988, Dickson and Savill 1974, Farrell 1984). Fertilizer application should be researched and applied only as part of a comprehensive silvicultural management system; its use does not compensate for otherwise poor management practices. Maximum returns from fertilizer application are realized when they are properly integrated with other silvicultural activities (e.g. Duryea and Dougherty 1990, Simpson and Grant 1991), requiring foliar leaf monitoring of nutrient status, especially up to the time of canopy closure.

Pest and disease management Although fears are often expressed for the ecological stability of plantation forests (see Zobel *et al.* 1987), well-adapted, well-managed stands seldom experience to epidemics of pests or diseases (Bain 1981, Chou 1981, Whitehead 1981, 1982). Large-scale pest or disease problems usually demonstrate neglect or ignorance of the advice of geneticists, entomologists, and pathologists (e.g. *Heteropsylla cubana* damage to *Leucaena leucocephala* in Asia; Hughes 1989), or the limitations of the tree species for plantation culture (e.g. *Conifericoccus agathidis* damage to *Agathis robusta* in sub-tropical eastern Australia; Queensland Department of Forestry 1987; *Cinara cupressi* damage to *Cupressus lusitanica* in southern Africa; Barnes 1992), or the failure of some aspect of management. They may therefore be addressed by use of a broader range of genetic material (e.g. *Leucaena*; Hughes 1989), a closer matching of genetic material to site (e.g. *Pinus radiata* susceptibility to *Dothistroma septospora* in Australasia; Simpson and Ades 1990), cultural practices which ensure that stands are maintained in a vigorous condition (e.g. *Sirex noctilio* damage to *P radiata* in Australia; Haugen 1990), or basic hygiene practices (e.g. application of urea to cut conifer stumps to prevent infection by *Heterobasidion annosum*; Hibberd 1991). Risks are certainly greatest for clonal plantations; selection for pest and disease resistance is already emphasized in these cases. Poplar breeding programmes, for example, first screen for resistance to *Marssonia*, *Melampsora*, and *Dothiciza*; only resistant families or individuals are then tested for production and quality traits.

Effective protection against plantation pests and diseases can be achieved only through an understanding of the biology of the species, and the development and application of systems which integrate measures such as quarantine, surveillance and control (e.g. Hosking and Gadgil 1987, Manion 1991, Speight and Wainhouse 1989). An important element of a protection strategy is to design the plantation estate as a mosaic of age classes and, if possible, species: plantation crops tend to be vulnerable to different agents at different stages of their life cycles. Such a strategy usually has other advantages, in terms of aesthetic, conservation, and recreation values, and the heterogeneity confers a measure of resilience which enables forests to persist despite environmental fluctuations, biological hazards, and changing demands (Malcolm 1979). Though it may be difficult to create such heterogeneity initially, it should be an explicit objective of management as plantations develop (e.g. Evans 1992).

Fire protection and management Forest fires are natural phenomena in many parts of the world; many ecosystems have evolved with fires and are resilient to, or even dependent on, them. Many plantation crops, however, are susceptible to fire, especially at early ages, and a fire management and control strategy is therefore a necessary part of most plantation forestry operations. Plantations should be designed to facilitate fire protection and suppression; monitoring of both weather and quantities of combustible fuel is necessary to predict fire risk. Fuel load reduction by low-intensity controlled burning is possible and desirable in many cases; efficient communications, reporting and suppression strategies are necessary, and are operational in many plantation programmes (e.g. Fuller 1991, Lear and Waldrop 1990, Pyne 1984).

Spacing, thinning and pruning

Total biomass production per unit area is determined largely by the species, site and climate. However, the allocation of wood between stem and branches, its distribution between fewer, larger stems or more numerous smaller stems, and its quality, are to a large extent under the forester's control, through the choice of spacing, thinning and pruning regimes. The interaction of these regimes with species and site determines the potential end uses and, therefore, the profitability of the plantation crop. Most commercial plantation regimes are now determined by economic criteria applied to stand models which predict product yields (e.g. Leuschner 1990, Whyte 1989). Regimes may therefore vary widely, according to intended products and markets.

For example, plantation establishment stockings range from as few as 250 plants per hectare (e.g. 'direct' sawlog regimes for *Pinus radiata* in New Zealand) to as many as 40,000 (e.g. *Pinus sylvestris* in parts of continental Europe). Common establishment stockings range from 1,000 to 2,500 trees per hectare. Thinning and pruning regimes depend on species, initial stocking, and intended end product (e.g. Evans 1992, Savill and Evans 1986). Thinning is particularly important where sawn-timber or veneer are being produced, as is pruning to reduce the extent of knots. In many cases, however, it has been neglected due to economic or operational constraints, and the quality and value of the plantation crop have suffered as a result.

Harvesting and regeneration

The rotation length (the period from establishment to final harvest) is determined by the products for which the plantation is grown, climate and site characteristics, and by economic criteria; most plantation crops are managed on rotations of between thirty and sixty years. Rotations for pole and pulp production are shortest: current minima are around five years for poles (*Casuarina*, south-east India; Kondas, 1981) and seven to eight years for pulp (*E globulus*, Portugal; Pereira and Santos Pereira 1988; *Eucalyptus* hybrids, Brazil and the Congo; Camphinos and Ikemori 1989, Delwaulle 1985). Where plantations are grown for sawn-timber and veneer production, rotation periods vary from around twenty years to well in excess of a hundred years.

Harvesting techniques range from essentially manual to completely mechanized; those appropriate in any given case will depend on economic and environmental parameters. Due to rapid developments in technology and machinery, there is a substantial, if somewhat ephemeral, literature (e.g. FAO 1987, FERIC 1991, Staaf and Wiksten 1984). The system must maintain site and environmental quality, and be compatible with requirements for regeneration or restocking of the site. In many short rotation plantation crops, species which can be regenerated from coppice (i.e. regrowth from the cut base of the tree) are preferred to those which cannot, although the merits of coppice management will depend on costs and returns from it relative to those associated with the ability to restock with genetically superior plants (e.g. Pereira and Santos Pereira 1988). In many plantation programmes, techniques developed for initial site preparation and establishment have not proved transferable to subsequent rotations because of altered site conditions. Substantial research and development efforts have been necessary to adapt to these new conditions (e.g. Boardman 1988, Hibberd 1991, Queensland Department of Forestry 1989).

Sustainable plantation forestry

Successful plantation forestry depends, therefore, on the coordinated application of an array of technical elements, integrated within the broader economic, social and cultural contexts. Each plantation is to some extent unique and site-specific, but is also subject to many uncertainties during its rotation. Whilst the fundamental principles of successful plantation forestry are well established, their successful application to particular situations requires informed interpretation and intelligent adaptation. Successful plantation forestry is characterized by substantial and sustained research and development efforts specific to the particular plantation programme. It is clear to us, however – as it was to Byron and Waugh (1988) or Romm (1989) in the case of forest resources more generally – that issues of political economy are far more important determinants of the nature and success of plantation programmes than are issues which are primarily technical.

Unfortunately, assessments of forestry development projects typically focus on financial and technical impacts rather than on their broader consequences in environmental, institutional and social terms (Barnes and Olivares 1988). Analyses of plantation forestry proposals or practices should, therefore, first address these broader issues; it is only then that appropriate scientific and technical interventions can be defined.

Improving plantation forestry

The first two sections of this chapter have outlined the nature, contexts and practice of plantation forestry. This section discusses how plantation forestry might be improved, in terms of both its role within societies and economies, and its technical practice.

Simple plantation forestry

'Plantation forestry' has come to imply relatively intensive management of simplified forest systems for a range of wood products. In terms of wood increment per unit area, well-managed simple plantations are many times more productive than most natural forests, and the plantation forests of many countries are now a major component of their productive forest resources. The financial returns from these plantations can compare favourably to those from alternative, sustainable, land uses.

Such plantation forestry is relatively demanding of resources. Consequently, it is increasingly concentrated on those sites which are inherently most productive, and at which environmental and social values are least likely to be prejudiced. In effect, this implies less extensive, more intensive plantation programmes, concentrated in countries where the forest land base is stable and secure and inputs can be readily assured (Bingham 1985, Gauthier 1991).

Complex plantation forestry

In many other circumstances, plantation forestry will have a broader and more integrated role. This more complex form of plantation forestry will be distinguished by objectives, species, management regimes and tenure arrangements other than those typical of simple plantation forestry. Its major characteristics are likely to include:

1. A more intimate association with other land uses. Simple plantation forestry is typified by a sharp distinction between plantation forest and other land uses. The 'boundary' between plantation forest and agricultural use will become less distinct as plantation forestry becomes more complex. The various taungya systems, widely practised as means of afforestation in the tropics (Evans 1992), are an example of this complexity in the early stages of plantation forestry.
2. More direct involvement of local people in the conception and implementation of plantation forestry, and in the sharing of its benefits and products. Simple plantation forestry has been characterized by the limited involvement, for example as wage labour, or exclusion, of local people (e.g. Douglas 1983). There is increasing understanding of how participatory planning, management and use might be developed and practised (e.g. Arnold and Stewart 1991, FAO 1985a, Griffin 1988), and this approach now characterizes some programmes involving plantation forestry (e.g. Gilmour *et al.* 1989, Arnold and Stewart 1991, Sargent 1990).
3. More complex species composition and plantation structure. Simple plantation forests are typically even-aged monocultures, producing similar products discontinuously. Complex plantation forests are likely to comprise more intimate mixtures of species, yielding a more continuous flow of more diverse products. This does not necessarily imply that tree species will be grown together as polycultures, though this will be appropriate in particular circumstances. In others, a mosaic of relatively small blocks of tree species may be more easily managed, but still yield the desired variety of products.

The greatest challenge to the adoption of complex plantation forestry is probably the necessary conceptual change, or 'paradigm shift' (Gilmour *et al.* 1989), on the part of policy makers and forest managers. There is, however, encouraging evidence of rapidly increasing awareness of the diverse potentials of complex plantation forestry, as the four examples below illustrate:

1. The proposals by Sargent and her colleagues (1990) for complex plantation forestry on degraded but heavily farmed sites in the Khun Song Forest Reserve, Thailand, arose from plans for *Eucalyptus* afforestation for pulp production. Plantation forestry could only succeed by providing sustainable land use of direct benefit to local

people; consequently, a variety of tenure arrangements and agroforestry practices were incorporated into the plantation planning and design process, and the pulpwood crop was integrated into agricultural production systems of immediate value to farmers.

2. Similarly, Spanish *Eucalyptus* plantation forests are now being designed and managed to facilitate a range of agroforestry practices for e.g. sawntimber, honey and eucalyptus oil, in addition to pulpwood (Wilson 1992).

3. Britain's new National Forest and Community Forests are based around plantation forests managed for wood production, but with major emphasis on recreational use, amenity and conservation values (Countryside and Forestry Commissions 1991).

4. Elsewhere, simple plantation forests may be managed in a way which will gradually increase species diversity and the range of products. The Nepalese example described by Gilmour *et al.* (1990) is such a case, which may have relevance in many subsistence economies. Sites available for plantation establishment in Nepal's middle hills are highly degraded, and *Pinus* species are among the few able to establish successfully. However, silvicultural manipulation may be designed to favour native broadleaved species, which are able to regenerate under the pine canopy. The stand may thereby ultimately be dominated by broadleaves, the products of which are more directly useful to local people.

Conclusions

The appropriate role and future prospects of plantation forestry vary between and within nations. Although there are prospects for global and regional coordination of forestry activities (e.g. Anon 1991), decisions about particular plantation forestry programmes can sensibly be made only at levels close to resource users (Romm 1991). Strategic reviews of plantation programmes and prospects are common at the national level (e.g. Liew That Chim 1984, Dargavel 1990), and provide a means to link international opportunities and concerns with local experiences, possibilities and constraints. The conclusions we draw below therefore provide only a general framework for policy determination, scientific research, and operational implementation, which should be given detail locally:

1. Plantation forestry is most appropriate where land and tree tenure are

not contentious, and where plantation systems can be managed sustainably to satisfy both industrial and non-industrial demands. Simple plantation forestry, emphasizing industrial wood production, will become increasingly concentrated on productive sites close to processing facilities, in nations whose economies are perceived to be relatively stable.

2. In many other circumstances, in both industrialized and less-industrialized economies, investment in complex plantation forestry is more likely to satisfy societies' demands from forest resources than is investment in simpler systems. This implies a redefinition of the objectives and principles of plantation forestry, to describe a more integrated form of land use yielding a wider range of products.

3. Proposals for plantation forestry should therefore be formulated in the broader social context. Participatory methodologies developed for agroforestry interventions offer some guidance to how this might be achieved. The assessment of social and environmental impacts, and their acceptance by those affected, are prerequisites for successful plantation forestry.

4. Decisions about investments in plantation forestry should be guided by broad economic assessments of plantation performance and alternatives, rather than by the narrow financial analyses often applied in the past. The evolving economic appreciation of the elements of sustainable development has much to contribute towards this end.

5. The conceptualization, planning and implementation of plantation forestry programmes must emphasize flexibility and adaptability, which should also characterize the terms of finance for plantations.

6. Integrated, interdisciplinary research is fundamental to successful plantation forestry, both prior to plantation design and establishment, and throughout the plantation life cycle. Such research would define the economic, social and environmental contexts of possible plantation forests, explore indigenous knowledge, and draw from the substantial body of scientific and technical information already acquired in most regions. The integration of agroforestry and plantation forestry methodologies and technologies may be particularly valuable.

7. Well-qualified, well-motivated, competent and imaginative operational staff, sensitive to local demands and expectations, are essential for sustainable plantation forestry, particularly as it becomes more complex. Their education and training should emphasize skills in the recognition and analysis of issues and problems, as well as scientific understanding and technical competence.

8. Adequate genetic resources of potentially useful species are the biological basis of plantation forestry. Efforts to enhance their *in situ* and *ex situ* conservation, their availability, and their improvement, are important to ensure the flexibility necessary for plantation forests to respond to changing demands and pressures.

The relatively short history of plantation forestry has been characterized by a focus on the scientific and technical requirements for wood production, which have been successfully developed and implemented in many cases. Often, however, the economic, environmental and social consequences of plantation forestry programmes have been less than fully emphasized. The potential contribution of plantation forestry to most societies can be realized only if its purposes are broadened, and its practice more integrated with other land uses. The challenge ahead is, therefore, to build on the considerable body of experience and information relevant to plantation forestry, and direct it towards a broader range of objectives and practices than those which have been common in the past.

BOX 6.1
Plantations of indigenous tree species in Ghana

In Ghana, there have been variable successes with the establishment and growth of plantations of indigenous tree species. A study was recently completed for the International Tropical Timber Organization (ITTO), based on information documented since the 1930s. Most early work was for trial purposes, or to provide opportunities for taungya cropping to villagers living near forest reserves. Tree planting increased in the 1960s and 1970s, when the species planted included *Khaya ivorensis, Khaya anthotheca, Entandophragma spp.,Terminalia ivorensis, Tieghemella heckellii, Tarrietia utilis, Mansonia altissima* and *Triplochiton scleroxylon,* either in pure plantation or under a mixed taungya system. There are currently about 10,500 hectares under indigenous plantation, and the most successful species have been *Mansonia altissima, Triplochiton scleroxylon* and *Terminalia ivorensis.*

However, plantations have been more or less limited to forest reserves, because of conflicting agricultural demands for land outside reserves, and farmers have been reluctant to plant trees because there is no secure tenure for trees privately planted. Furthermore, although the area of plantation establishment is well documented, the area of failed

---

plantations is not known; it is thought that there has been considerable replacement of indigenous species with non-native fast-growing species. The ITTO report suggests that the reasons for lack of success include:

- damage and loss due to fire;
- lack of appropriate inputs for maintenance;
- poor planting stock, and poor survival after transplanting;
- lack of research information and silvicultural knowledge about indigenous species;
- problems with seed collection and viability;
- inadequate management and supervision;
- incidence of pests and diseases, especially with species in the *Meliaceae* and with *Terminalia ivorensis*, *Pericopsis elata* and *Khaya spp*;
- poor site selection;
- improper definition of objectives in terms of end uses.

C.S.

Source: Forestry Research Institute of Ghana. Pre-Project Report to the International Tropical Timber Organization on: *Manmade Forests of Indigenous Species: A systematic preparation to industrial tree plantations in Ghana* (1991).

BOX 6.2
Plantations in Costa Rica

Since 1979, a range of incentives for reforestation by plantation have been made available by the Costa Rican government. By 1989 these had encouraged the reforestation of some 36,000 hectares on private land. Although initial incentive schemes based on tax deductions were naturally only attractive to payers of significant amounts of tax, other schemes currently give incentives to owners of small and medium landholdings, other individuals or organized groups.

A reforestation programme is desirable from various standpoints. However, its success should not be measured only in terms of the area planted. Serious problems have affected the quality of reforestation activities in Costa Rica, which may greatly reduce the plantation contribution to the forest-based industrial development sought in the medium term. The following issues are of particular concern:

- the restricted range of officially approved species and frequent failure to match species to site;
- the insufficient supply of seed from known good sources with quality control, leading to frequent use of poor quality seed;
- the lack of demand for plantation products, stemming from both the inability of existing industry to process small-diameter logs, and market conservatism with respect to species. It is unfortunate that one of the few planted species for which a strong demand exists, *Cordia alliodora*, has proved to be one of the biggest failures in plantations;
- the distribution of many reforested areas in small blocks over a large number of private holdings, with consequent high costs for logging and transport to existing processing centres.

C.S.

Source: Finegan, B. and Reiche, C., Tropical Forestry Action Plan Costa Rica. ODA Forestry Action Programme: Integrated Natural Forest Management Project, Project Proposal, unpublished (1992).

BOX 6.3
Development assistance for plantations

Forest-based industrial development is one of five fields of action of the Tropical Forest Action Programme and, although other activities are included, the field is dominated by industrial plantation establishment and management.

A biennial review of international cooperation in tropical forestry is prepared by the FAO for the Committee on Forest Development in the Tropics. The review shows that assistance to forest-based industrial development increased from US$ 109.6 million in 1986, to US$ 191.9 million in 1988, and to US$ 347.6 million in 1990 (the most recent data available). This increase is more than threefold over the six-year period.

It is interesting to note that, during the same period, there was a decrease in official development aid for fuelwood plantations from US$ 100.8 million to US$ 74.7 million. This is despite predictions, supported by local data, indicating that the relative proportion of non-industrial plantations would increase. Development assistance data are notoriously difficult to assemble accurately; however, in this case it is thought that funds for fuelwood plantations have been reclassified and included in the

TFAP field 'forestry in land use,' with the realization by donors that communities establish plantations with objectives other than fuelwood alone. It is, however, fairly certain that the relative proportion of non-industrial to industrial plantations has increased since 1980.

C.S.

Principal source: Ball, J.B., *Forest Plantations and the Wise Management of Tropical Forests*, Paper read to Oxford Forestry Institute Conference on 'The Wise Management of Tropical Forests' (1992).

BOX 6.4
The United Kingdom Overseas Development Administration's approach to plantations

The following is quoted from the United Kingdom Overseas Development Administration's Environmental Manual:

Afforestation and reforestation

'Compared with the destruction of forests, planting trees has many positive effects on the environment. Nevertheless, the following possible adverse effects need to be noted:

i.   Depletion of groundwater. Trees intercept rainfall and have a large appetite for groundwater which disappears in evapotranspiration. They can lower the surrounding water-table, which might be to the detriment of other species, wells and agriculture, although species vary widely in this respect.
ii. Trees provide a habitat for pests, predators and disease vectors, as well as for beneficient animals.
iii. Forests may increase the risk of fire.
iv. The introduction of new tree species, or changing the balance between existing ones, will tend to alter the ecosystem.
v.   Fast-growing pioneer species whose valuable attributes, such as ability to colonize deforested and degraded land, may be offset by less desirable traits. These include reduction of soil moisture/soil fertility, suppression of other vegetation, and invasiveness (i.e. tendency to invade farmlands or replace natural vegetation). Care is

needed in matching species to local needs and site conditions to ensure that the benefits outweigh any such disadvantages.

vi. Owners of commercial plantations usually debar local people and their animals, or severely restrict the use that locals can make of the forest. Women may be particularly affected by such restrictions.

Some of these problems can be mitigated by proper forest management and planning. Controlled planting, cutting and spacing can minimize fire risks, prevent the crowding out of other species, etc. The careful and appropriate choice of species can help retain ecological balance and introduce variety into the landscape. Promoting social forestry can help compensate local people for the loss of access to a forest resource.'

CHAPTER 7

CONCLUSIONS

Stephen M.J. Bass and Caroline Sargent

Plantations interacting with society

Industrial plantations have had only a short and discontinuous history of supplying wood, confined largely to the latter half of the twentieth century. Plantations have been established in response to political and economic imperatives for increasing forest resources, wherever natural forests are inadequate or have been depleted.

Industrial plantations, at their best, have been major contributors to local socioeconomic development. They have provided raw materials, infrastructure, employment, income, and environmental and recreational services for local people. Wood, in particular, has been a basic material for development in all its 'stages'; and *per caput* wood requirements have tended to increase as nations have developed. Plantations which have contributed positively to local socioeconomic development have been established on land with few competing demands, in circumstances which, locally, have been politically uncontentious.

At their worst, industrial plantations have taken land out of food production in areas of acute food shortage, they have dislocated people and ignored indigenous use rights, and they have degraded culturally important wild populations of plants and animals, habitats and landscapes. Such plantations have invariably have been designed and implemented with a 'top-down' perspective, ignoring local needs, local values and local rights.

The choice of whether and where to establish industrial plantations should be about the best use of land within local political, industrial, social and environmental contexts. In practice, however, those who control land and industry have been free to make decisions irrespective of local needs and desires.

The potential instability of plantations caused by genetic uniformity is widely recognized; it has been the downfall of certain plantations – though not a great many – when faced with pest and disease outbreaks. However, a further dimension to instability, based on political and social acceptability, is perhaps more significant. Plantations which are established for narrow purposes, and are imposed on local people, tend to be those that have failed most dramatically. The high visibility of such mistakes in the earlier plantation developments of the twentieth century has meant that the public retains generally unfavourable impressions of plantations.

The extent of society's interactions with plantations depends on:

- the **size** of the plantation and its component stands;
- the plantation's **boundary configuration** with respect to adjacent land uses;
- the degree of **competition for land**;
- the **rate** of plantation establishment;
- the particular **type and objectives** of the plantation;
- the degree of **lifestyle change** that the plantation objectives will entail;
- the **balance of power** between local people and any outside plantation developer, notably concerning the ownership of the plantation and access/use rights.

Factors that encourage plantations

Many policy and economic signals will encourage investment in plantations. This does not mean to say, however, that all such investment will be socially desirable (the preconditions for sustainable plantations, including the requirements for communicating the **right** policy and economic signals, are considered later in these conclusions).

Once natural forests become overexploited, and remaining forest resources are economically inaccessible, industrial investment in plantations will tend to be favoured. Where people are excluded from natural forests, notably by land enclosure, they may also be obliged to plant, in order to secure their wood supplies elsewhere. The availability of (poorer quality) land, for which there are no politically contentious competing uses, will foster planting by both industrial and local groups (although industrial groups have often not restricted themselves to such land – hence the social problems associated with plantations). The rate of planting will depend upon many factors. However, strategic imperatives to build up wood supplies, notably after war, have resulted in some of the most massive and rapid planting efforts.

Given the dominance of major corporations in large wood-using industries, there is much competitive pressure to ensure continuous, high-quality, uniform supplies of wood at low cost to supply mass markets. It is not, therefore, surprising that corporations have also become involved in plantations. Strong, stable and growing markets for large quantities of uniform wood products have encouraged major industrial planting in the last forty years. Such investment has been made possible only by the availability of investment finance at low opportunity cost; and by official incentives and promotion of planting, especially tax arrangements, favouring forestry.

Long-term stability, in policies and authorities that affect forestry and long-term investment, helps to encourage a strong plantation resource. Low inflation, protection from high interest rates and undue taxes on land, and stability in interest rates, taxes, market and trade conditions, are all conducive to plantations, as is secure and unambiguous tenure of land available for planting. However, such stability has been comparatively rare in many countries – hence the discontinuity in plantation invest-ments. There have been many isolated plantation investments that have taken advantage of ephemeral tax policies in particular.

The general working approaches of agencies involved in official development planning, aid and finance have tended to favour plantations, which are easier to plan and operate than the more uncertain natural forest management.

Factors that discourage plantations

The continued availability of forest products from natural forests, at lower cost than those from plantations, has discouraged investment in plan-tations. This would be acceptable, were it not for the fact that, in the tropics, natural forest products are undervalued. Hence their preferential removal has tended to be at excessive rates, which has damaged those important natural forest services such as biodiversity conservation and watershed protection, that depend upon natural forests remaining intact.

The availability of cheap wood imports also discourages plantations. Again, this has been acceptable, except where policies that encourage imports, as opposed to home production, send economic signals which encourage unsustainable forestry in the exporting country.

The high price of capital in many rapidly-developing economies has tended to delay plantation establishment. This is especially the case where the cost of clearing land to establish plantations is high. This, however, has also predisposed developers to establish plantations by liquidating high-value natural forests, in order to raise immediate revenue.

Plantation policies have fluctuated, often wildly, over the last century. This has not provided the stability required to establish a balanced plantation resource capable of sustaining yields over the years. Such inconsistencies in policy stem in part from the inability to deal with the uncertainties associated with plantations. These are similar to the uncertainties connected to agriculture, except that they extend further into the future, and hence encompass a much wider range of unknowns:

- difficulties in assessing future markets and forecasting demands;
- uncertainties about technology changes and the consequent demands for wood;
- changing assessments of the silvicultural possibilities of producing products of the desired quality;
- hence, changing assessments of the economic viability of plantations over the rotation;
- and, today especially, concern about changing climatic and pollution conditions over the life of a plantation crop.

Many land-use policies have tended to favour risk reduction, and the gain of more immediate benefits. In particular, they have favoured short-term agricultural production on cleared land. This has discouraged plantations; although in future there should be possibilities for combining agricultural and forestry needs in risk-minimizing, complex agroforestry systems.

Plantations *vis-à-vis* natural forests

Industrial plantations offer many particular advantages over natural forests:

- the ability to select the forest **location** and therefore to take advantage of climate and soil (the most critical factors for tree productivity), infrastructure, transport and labour opportunities;
- the greater ability, relative to natural forests, to **protect the boundaries and control the use** of plantations. Other things being equal, investment will preferentially be attracted to plantations.
- the ability to pre-determine **fibre supply characteristics** through species/variety selection;
- the **ability to apply 'industrial' techniques** to better regulate input and output in circumstances of bulk demand and industrial imperatives for efficiency – and hence to produce socially desirable products at the lowest possible cost.

However, plantations are not substitutes for natural forests. In natural forests, biological diversity confers resilience and stability, and provides multiple benefits for local people – particularly in times of seasonal shortages and occasional catastrophe. Such resilience is barely present in plantations. The term 'reforestation' can hence be misleading if it means tree planting as a way to recoup losses of natural forest. A different form of forest will result, and will produce different, and narrower, benefits. Plantations can, therefore, be only a partial answer to deforestation.

Industrial plantations, on the other hand, are **complements** to natural forest. They can be additive and supportive in much the same way that agriculture is. Unlike natural forests, plantation productivity and management impacts are relatively easy to predict. Where wood or biomass productivity is their principal purpose, they are intentionally unstable, because this is ecologically necessary in order to realize high growth rates. Fast-growing plantations can, however, be structured in more complex ways, to provide certain additional social, biological and environmental benefits; however, their management will similarly be more complex.

Plantations can, in certain circumstances, directly assist natural forest management. Where inputs are lowered, plantations will generally move towards a more natural (diverse) state. They can therefore assist land/ forest restoration and rehabilitation. The costs of doing this will be considered prohibitive by policy-makers, however, if the various values of natural forests remain unrecognized. More usually, and because plantations have a higher perceived and more easily-realizable economic value than natural forest, plantations have contributed to the **loss** of the natural resource, for plantations themselves have been established by **removing** natural forest. Occasionally, however, plantations have acted as effective buffers to natural forest removal – but this has depended upon very specific circumstances, and the buffer effect cannot be said to be general. Protection of natural forest can only be achieved through policies and practices which attribute higher values to natural forest in relation to alternative land uses, including agriculture and plantation.

In order to achieve complementary relationships between plantations and natural forests, the establishment of plantations should not, by competition, detract from the realizable and recognized values of natural forests on which their continued survival depends. Only when the confusion between the functions and benefits of plantations and natural forests are clearly recognized by those who influence policy making and planning, will rational forest land use – based on the integration and prioritization of specific values – be achieved.

Where plantations are appropriate

Plantation forestry is most appropriate where it **adds value**. The challenge is to add value for local people, at the same time as adding value in terms of the industrial produce which more usually supplies far-off needs. The difficulty in achieving such a balance is compounded by the many competing demands for land experienced in many parts of the world today, and by the requirement that plantations be secure in a given location for a very long period. Plantations are therefore more likely to be appropriate where land and tree tenure are not contentious, where there is no great flux in land use, and where plantation systems can be managed sustainably to satisfy both industrial and non-industrial demands.

Plantations have been appropriate for a range of value-added purposes, producing:

* wood and cellulose for industrial development;
* industrial energy (wood gas and ethanol);
* domestic energy (firewood and charcoal);
* rural employment;
* environmental services to help maintain agriculture;
* environmental protection and rehabilitation;
* income, especially over the long term;
* capital growth; and
* reinforcing tenure rights.

Sustainable plantation forms have included:

* **industrial plantations** providing a proportion of the **wood harvest to local people**;
* **industrial plantations** with **multi-purpose trees** as a component, and guaranteed public/community access;
* **small plantation blocks within a farm system**, usually as **outgrower** plantations;
* **silvi-pastoral systems** in which commercial wood production and local grazing are combined;
* **agroforestry systems** in which wood production and agricultural crops are combined;
* **integral taungya systems**, where a large forestry plantation resource is built up by phasing many small participatory forestry operations;
* **tree tenure forestry**, where landless or poor farmers establish plantations on state land allocated to them specifically for tree growing;

• forms of plantation that can accommodate **recreation/amenity** requirements.

Where plantations are inappropriate

Plantations are likely to be **inappropriate** where they are established on
land of higher value for other social, environmental or economic purposes.
This is especially the case where this is done by compulsory acquisition
(incurring high social costs in particular) or by clearing natural forests
(incurring high environmental costs). Plantations will also be inappropriate where rapid land-use changes are both expected and desired by
society, and hence high costs are associated with keeping land under a tree
crop for many years.

Global and national estimates for tree planting requirements have
tended to be made with a top-down perspective on local needs which, as
we have discussed, has led to many social and economic problems. There is
a danger that this trend may be exacerbated by current notions of
establishing vast areas of 'carbonforest' to offset increased emissions of
carbon dioxide from burning fossil fuels. The effect of tree plantations on
global carbon dioxide can be only limited and temporary. Given conflicting social and agricultural needs for land, the large-scale establishment of
'carbonforest' in the tropics at rates promoted by the Noordwijk Convention will be neither feasible nor desirable. Strategies for carbon sequestration and storage should focus on wise use and protection of natural
forest, and on encouraging tree growth within the agricultural landscape.

In contrast, there are currently few mechanisms and means to encourage plantation schemes that address local needs, but which also take
advantage of national and international markets for forest produce. Some
of the better outgrower schemes and forest village organizations have
been able to do this. Greater attention needs to be given to devising more
appropriate local roles, and allying these, to mutual advantage, with
reviewing the roles of government.

Preconditions for sustainable plantations

Guidelines

From the above discussions, we can suggest certain guidelines for the establishment of plantations which are commercially viable, and yet which also play further sustainable roles in society. These guidelines are generally applicable, but focus on the tropics. They are not, however, intended to be comprehensive or definitive.

Policy

A coordinated and stable (national) land-use policy and plan will increasingly be necessary. In them, forestry should be treated as more than a residual land use, and the relative roles of natural forests and plantations should be well defined.

Policy frameworks need to be especially clear about plantation forestry's relationships with other forms of land use, notably natural forests and agriculture. Generally, natural forests and plantations should be considered as separate but related concerns. Only then will policy ambiguities about their substitutability be removed. As we have seen, all the policies that pertain to plantations and their alternatives and complements must be stable – financial and tenurial policies especially.

Wherever policy **has** been improved – and this has been witnessed in many countries in the last several years – the most critical requirement will be for techniques and incentives to implement the improved policy. Increased public participation will be the greatest challenge.

Legislation

The framework of land laws, and its practical enforceability, are particularly important in determining whether plantations are viable. Ownership and use rights should be clear before any plantation scheme is begun; and uncodified – but none the less socially legitimate – rights and privileges must be identified and respected.

Assessment of actual or potential plantations

Decisions about investments in industrial plantations should be guided by broad economic assessments of plantations and alternatives, rather than by the narrow financial analyses applied in the past. The evolving understanding of the preconditions for sustainable development has much to contribute towards this end. Individual plantation developments should aim to successfully meet industrial objectives, whilst also forming an integral part of the local society, economy and landscape. This will necessitate an approach which treats social and cultural factors as seriously as economic and technical factors, at all stages of the plantation development process. A **sustainable** plantation development might therefore be defined as one which:

- is commercially viable;
- increases social benefits from a given stock of resources, notably land;
- increases the stock of resources, notably woody biomass;
- promotes social development;
- promotes economic development;
- contributes to poverty reduction;
- builds on local cultural traditions;
- expands employment, especially locally;
- includes the positive participation of local people – and especially minority groups, indigenous people and women – and accommodates their needs;
- does not adversely affect the environment and biodiversity, and where possible mends environmental damage;
- increases resilience, through incorporating biological and structural diversity;
- minimizes the use of external inputs;
- distributes the costs and benefits of the plantation equitably, including all externalities.

Industrial involvement in plantations

Industry will inevitably be involved in plantation development, because of the extensive economic links between the industrial sector and plantation forest products, especially wood. Corporations are best able to realize economies of scale and apply the necessary assets to the large task of clearing land, establishing trees, and managing them over several years. They have the ability to work competitively in the marketplace, and hence to improve the efficiency of resource use. There are many opportunities to improve competitiveness in large-scale plantation forestry through introducing more efficient technology, production management and marketing. There is particular scope in developing countries, where the level of mechanization is currently low and technology is out of date, yet environmental and labour factors are promising. Corporations are usually better able than governments to increase competitiveness and efficiency in this way.

Technical practice

Plantations require relatively intensive, but flexible, management if they are to succeed. The integration of many specific plantation forestry technical practices into a coordinated and adaptable system is critical for the success of a particular plantation. Foresters continually have to choose between different silvicultural and management techniques to achieve different mixes of goods and services from specific forest areas in changing circumstances; no single mix can be recommended as ideal for a given situation. Where the necessary resources and management expertise are available, the productive capacity of plantations is unlikely to be rivalled by natural forests. Where such resources are less certain, however, the expectations of plantations should be lower; and plantations may not even be appropriate.

Integrated research

Integrated, interdisciplinary research is fundamental to successful industrial plantation forestry, both prior to plantation establishment, and throughout successive rotations. The relatively short history of plantation forestry has been characterized by a focus on the scientific and technical requirements for wood production. These have been successfully developed and implemented in many cases. The full potential of biotechnology, however, has barely been exploited; there are considerable constraints to its widespread use, and results have so far been disappointing. New, interdisciplinary research would analyse the economic, social and environmental contexts of possible plantation forests, explore and incorporate indigenous knowledge, and draw from the substantial body of scientific and technical information already acquired in most regions of the world. The integration of agroforestry and plantation forestry technologies may be particularly valuable. This is especially the case for complex plantations.

Genetic resources

Adequate genetic resources of potentially useful species form the biological basis of plantation forestry. A considerable (perhaps tenfold) increase in the number of species included in genetic conservation programmes is recommended. Efforts to enhance their *in situ* and *ex situ* conservation status, their availability, and their improvement, are important to ensure the flexibility necessary for plantation forests to respond to changing demands and pressures.

Staff

Well-qualified, motivated, competent and imaginative operational staff, sensitive to local demands and expectations, are essential. This will particularly be the case as plantation forestry becomes more complex. Staff education and training should emphasize skills in participation, and in identifying and analysing issues and problems, as well as the scientific and technical competence necessary to raise, establish, maintain and monitor plantations.

Participation and terms of partnership

The participation of local people should be secured from the beginning of any potential plantation project, using Participatory/Rapid Rural Appraisal (P/RRA) and other participation techniques. Participation should continue throughout the project, in its management, monitoring and marketing. Good information availability and well-managed dialogue with affected communities will be key to avoiding the social/cultural problems that have plagued plantations in the past.

Improved understanding of social issues will be achieved by identifying and accommodating social complexity: consulting the relevant social groups; identifying their predispositions, their motivations and their perceptions of the values of trees and plantations, and assessing their control systems for maintaining these values. Participatory techniques will help in the process of negotiating appropriate balances of control over the plantation boundaries, objectives and operations and the distribution of costs and benefits. In general, local people will need a dominant influence in allocating land to forestry and in defining precise boundaries, and a strong role in plantation management, staffing, protection and monitoring.

Whatever the type of plantation chosen, most important is its **boundary** configuration with respect to neighbouring land uses. Plantation schemes may be far more acceptable locally if particular areas are excised because of their social or cultural value, or if the plantation edge is designed to provide social or environmental benefits, e.g. shelterbelts or recreation. Knowing where **not** to plant is as important as knowing where to plant.

Monitoring

Routine and detailed monitoring is required to keep track of the composition, physical condition, management status, use and impacts of plantations. The wider impacts of plantations should also be examined regularly, particularly their impacts on the protection and use of natural forests.

A future for plantations

In future, plantations will form an increasing proportion of forests. The predicted gap between industrial wood and cellulose requirements, and the supplies that will be available in many regions, is so large that only plantations can fill it cost-effectively. As Alf Leslie suggests in Chapter 4, a sustained increase of around 30 per cent in the current plantation rate, however, should be able to provide the expected world consumption of wood over the next century. Natural forests, in contrast, should principally be conserved; where appropriate, they may also be harvested for high quality and decorative timbers, and for multiple local goods, but only rarely for industrial wood and cellulose.

There is particular scope for realizing the comparative advantage of tropical country perennial cropping. Tree plantations can grow all year round at very high rates in the warm conditions of low latitudes, and require less cultivation of erodible soil than annual crops. Areas of the tropics and subtropics outside the arid and perhumid zones tend to have the most favourable climatic and soil conditions. Such comparative advantage can best be realized where there are no higher-valued uses for the land, which tends to exclude densely-populated areas.

Plantations can fill the predicted gap in supply, and realize the considerable comparative advantage in parts of the tropics and subtropics, while avoiding the many potential social, economic and ecological problems which have beset plantation forestry in the past. **Two approaches are appropriate for this**:

- One is **simple** plantations, treated as crops for meeting industrial wood demands, to be established in a favourable economic climate on land without alternative claims, close to the source of demand.
- The second is plantations of **complex** structure and/or purpose and/or set of users, to be established either by *de novo* design, or by being grown within natural forest; such plantations may be more appropriate in areas with many claims on land and many different types of forest benefits in demand.

Simple plantations are relatively demanding of resources. Consequently, investment will continue the trend of concentrating on those sites which are inherently most productive for industrial wood production; at which environmental and social values are least likely to be compromised; which are close to processing facilities; and which are in nations whose economies are perceived by investors to be relatively stable and where comparative advantage can be secured.

In many other circumstances – particularly where there are competing rights, needs and interests and land is scarce, where time horizons are short, or where demand for non-wood products and services is strong – an approach based on compromise is necessary. A broader range of plantation objectives and a more intimate integration with other land uses will then characterize successful plantations. There is scope for these more **complex plantations** in both industrialized and developing countries. Complex plantations will be composed of multiple species, for mixed uses or users, and be diverse in structure or age. They will also require improved access for the various users, through e.g. strategies giving common property or individual rights to defined components of the resource.

There is a further imperative for complex plantations. There are a great number of uncertainties facing forestry in the future – particularly climate change and the resulting fragility of genetically simple systems or monocultures, but also market uncertainties. To deal with uncertainty, plantations should be diverse, robust and resilient, whilst retaining their primary functions. To achieve this, the plantation estate may be constructed as a mosaic of age classes and, if possible, species; this may be done both *de novo* and within existing forest. Though it may be difficult to create such heterogeneity initially, especially on open or degraded sites, it should be an explicit objective of management as simple plantations develop. A strategy for resilience has other advantages, in terms of developing aesthetic, conservation and recreation values.

The trend towards complexity in plantations is not exclusive of a continued investment in simple plantations, wherever the latter may be appropriate. However, it does imply a redefinition of the objectives and principles of plantation forestry, to describe a more integrated form of land use yielding a wider range of products.

It will not be easy to locate the right balance in each type of complex plantation. In the longer term, increased cooperation between industry and communities in complex plantations may reveal their most appropriate respective roles. It should aid the internalization of the social and environmental externalities that so far have led to industrial plantations being condemned as the pariahs of forestry.

The social question is perhaps the key issue for tropical plantations in the next few decades. Given the clear need for mass-producing wood in vast quantities, large-scale industrial investment in plantations would seem desirable; and, indeed, its technical and financial efficacy has been borne out by historical experience. However, given the fact that a vast range of social purposes must be served **both** by that wood **and** by the intact forest ecosystem within which it is grown, there are now many imperatives for complexity in plantations and for greater societal control of plantations. On the face of it, small-scale (possibly traditional) 'craftsmanship' approaches would better achieve this than would large-scale industrial techniques. Plantation policies should, therefore, in future foster appropriate partnerships between people and industry; and industrial plantation practice should marry traditional forestry approaches and industrial techniques.

REFERENCES

Adlard, P. G., *Procedures for monitoring tree growth and site change* (Oxford: Oxford Forestry Institute, Tropical Forestry Papers 23, 1990).

Adlard, P. G., *Historical Background* Shell Tree Plantation Review Series, Study No. 1 (London: Shell International, 1992).

Alder, D. and T. J. Synott, *Permanent sample plot techniques for mixed tropical forest* (Oxford: Oxford Forestry Institute, Tropical Forestry Papers 25, 1992).

Aldhous, J. R., *Nursery practice* (London: HMSO, UK Forestry Commission Bulletin 43, 1972).

Allan, T. and J. P. Lanley, 'Global overview of status and trends of world's forests', in: *Proceedings of the technical workshop to explore options for global forest management*, (Bangkok, Thailand: IIED, ITTO, and ONEB, 1991).

Anon., *Proceedings of the 1985 Conference on Rapid Rural Appraisal* (Kohn Kaen University, Thailand, 1985).

Anon., *Proceedings of the technical workshop to explore options for global forest management* (Bangkok, Thailand: IIED, ITTO and ONEB, 1991).

Arnold, J. E. M., 'Economic considerations in agroforestry projects', *Agroforestry Systems* 1: 399–311 (1983).

Arnold, J. E. M., *Community forestry: ten years in review* (Rome: FAO Community Forestry Note 7, 1991).

Arnold, J. E. M., *Long term trends in global demand for and supply of industrial wood* (Oxford: Oxford Forestry Institute, 1991a).

Arnold, J. E. M., *Tree Products in agroecosystems: economic and policy issues*, Gatekeeper series no. 28. (London: IIED, 1991b).

Arnold, J. E. M. and W. C. Stewart, *Common property resource management in India* (Oxford: Oxford Forestry Institute, Tropical Forestry Papers 24, 1991).

Ascher, W. and R. G. Healy, *Natural resource policymaking in developing countries* (Durham, NC: Duke University Press, 1990).

Attiwell, P. M., 'Nutrient cycling in a *Eucalyptus obliqua* forest. III Growth, biomass and net primary production', *Australian Journal of Botany* 27, 439–458 (1979).

Bailly, C., C. Barbier, J. Clement, J. P. Goudet and O. Hamel, 'Les problèmes de la satisfaction des besoins en bois en Afrique tropicale sèche. Connaissances et incertitudes', *Bois et Forêts des Tropiques* 197: 23–43 (1982).

Bain, J., 'Forest monocultures – how safe are they? An entomologist's view', *New Zealand J Forestry* 26: 37–42 (1981).

Barbier, E. B., 'The concept of sustainable economic development', *Environmental Conservation* 14: 101–110 (1987).

Barbour, R. J. and R. M. Kellogg, 'Forest management and end-product quality: a Canadian perspective', *Canadian J Forest Research* **20**: 405–414 (1990).

Barnes, R. D., Personal communication (Oxford: Oxford Forestry Institute, 1992).

Barnes, R. D. and J. Burley, 'Vegetative propagation for improved tropical forest trees', Chapter 12 in: Abbott, A. J. and R. K. Atkin (eds), *Improving vegetatively propagated crops* (New York: Academic Press, 1987), pp. 211–227.

Barnes, D. F. and J. Olivares, *Sustainable resource management in agriculture and rural development projects: a review of bank policies, procedures and results* (Washington, DC: World Bank, 1988).

Barnes, R. D. and L. J. Mullin, 'The multiple population breeding strategy in Zimbabwe – five year results', in Gibson, G. L., A. R. Griffin and A. C. Matheson (eds), *Breeding tropical trees* (Oxford and Arlington, VA: Oxford Forestry Institute and Winrock International, 1989b), pp. 9–27.

Bass, S., *Sustainable forestry development in Northern Areas, Pakistan* (Gland, Switzerland: IUCN 1987).

Bass, S., *Social and Cultural Issues*, Shell Tree Plantation Review Series, Study No. 4. (London: Shell International Petroleum Company and World Wide Fund for Nature, 1992).

Beer de, J. H. and M. J. McDermott, *The economic value of non-timber forest products in Southeast Asia* (Amsterdam, Netherlands: Netherlands Committee for IUCN, Netherlands, 1989).

Behan, R. W., 'Multiresource forest management: a paradigmatic challenge to professional forestry', *J Forestry* **88**(4): 12–18 (1990).

Benezit, J. J., 'Soils and natural regeneration in Normandy', *Quarterly J Forestry* **85**: 30–36 (1991).

Bingham, C. W., 'Rationale for intensive forestry investment: a 1980s view', Chapter 2 in: Sedjo, R.A. (ed.), *Investment in forestry* (Boulder, CO: Westview Press, 1985), pp. 21–31.

Binkley, C. S. and J. R. Vincent, *Forest-based industrialization: a dynamic perspective*, World Bank Forest Policy Issues Paper, Washington DC (1990).

Binkley, C. S. and J. R. Vincent, 'Forest-based industrialization for economic development: a dynamic perspective'. Chapter 5 in: Sharma, N. P. (ed.), *Contemporary issues in forest management: policy implications* (Washington, DC: World Bank, 1992).

Binns, W. O., G. J. Mayhead and J. M. Mackenzie, *Nutrient deficiencies of conifers in British forests* (London: HMSO, UK Forestry Commission Leaflet 76, 1980).

Blair, H. W. and P. D. Olpadwala, 'Planning for appropriate forestry enterprises: lessons from rural development experience in Third World countries', *New Forests* **2**: 41–64 (1988).

Blatner, K. A. and J. L. Greene, 'Woodland owner attitudes toward timber production and management', *Resource management and optimization* 6: 205–233 (1989).

Boardman, R., 'Living on the edge – the development of silviculture in South Australian pine plantations', *Australian Forestry* 51: 135–156 (1988).

Boland, D. J. (ed.), *Trees for the tropics* (Canberra, Australia: ACIAR, 1989).

Booth, T. H., S. D. Searle and D. J. Boland, 'Bioclimatic analysis to assist performance selection for trials', *New Forests* 3: 225–234 (1989).

Borralho, N. M. G., P. P. Cotterill and P. J. Kanowski, 'Breeding objectives for pulp production of *Eucalyptus globulus* under different industrial cost structures', *Canadian J Forest Research* (in press).

Borralho, N. M. G., Personal communication (Obidos, Portugal: CELBI, 1992).

Brown, A. G., L. J. Wolf, P. A. Ryan and P. Voller, 'TREDAT: a tree crop data base', *Australian Forestry* 52: 23–29 (1989).

Brunig, E. F., M. von Buch, J. Heuveldop and K. F. Panzer, 'Stratification of the tropical moist forest for land use planning', in *Plant Research and Development*, vol. 2 (1975), pp. 21–44.

Brunig, E. F. and T. W. Schneider, *Forests and Microclimate: old neglects and new challenges*, Paper for the World Forestry Congress, Paris (1991).

Brunig, E. F., *Guidelines for Plantation Management* (Yokohama: ITTO, 1991).

Brunton, D. P., 'Financing small-scale rural manufacturing enterprises', in: *Small-scale forest-based processing enterprises* (Rome: Food and Agriculture Organization of the UN, Forestry Paper 79, 1987), pp. 117–148.

Burch, W. R., *Gods of the forest: myth, ritual and television in community forestry*, paper for Regional Community Forestry Training Centre, Bangkok (15–19 December 1987).

Burdon, R. D., 'Summing up', in: Gibson, G. L., A. R. Griffin and A. C. Matheson (eds), *Breeding tropical trees* (Oxford and Arlington, VA: Oxford Forestry Institute and Winrock International, 1989a), pp. 490–497.

Burdon, R. D., 'When is cloning on an operational scale appropriate?', in: Gibson, G. L., A. R. Griffin and A. C. Matheson (eds), *Breeding tropical trees* (Oxford and Arlington, VA: Oxford Forestry Institute and Winrock International, 1989b), pp. 9–27.

Byron, R. N. and G. Waugh, 'Forestry and fisheries in the Asian–Pacific region: issues in natural resource management', *Asian–Pacific Economic Literature* 2: 46–80 (1988).

Caldwell, L. K., *Between two worlds* (Cambridge: Cambridge University Press, 1990).

Cameron, J. N. and H. Lieshout, 'Realized gains for *P Radiata* from breeding and silvicultural developments introduced in the 1970s in Gippsland', in: Dieters, M. J. and D. G. Nikles (eds), *Proceedings, 10th Meeting of Research Working Group No. 1 of the Australian Forestry Council* (Gympie, Australia: Australian Forestry Council, 1988), pp. 198–204.

Cameron, J. L. and I. W. Penna, *The wood and the trees* (Melbourne, Australia: Australian Conservation Foundation, 1988).

Campbell, K., *An estimate of the carbon content of tropical forest plantations based on volume*, MSc Thesis, University of Wales, Bangor (1991).

Camphinos, E. Jr and Y. K. Ikemori, 'Selection and management of the basic population *Eucalyptus grandis* and *E urophylla* established at Aracruz for the long term breeding programme', from Barnes, R. D. and L. J. Mullen in Gibson *et al.* (1989b).

Cassells, D. S. and P. S. Valentine, 'From conflict to consensus – towards a framework for community control of the public forests and wildlands', *Australian Forestry* **51**: 47–56 (1988).

Caufield, C., *In the Rainforest*, London: Heinemann (1985).

Chambers, R., N. C. Saxena and T. Shah, *To the hands of the poor: water and trees* (New Delhi: Oxford and IBH Publishing Co. Pvt. Ltd, 1989).

Chambers, R., A. Pacey and L. Thrupp (eds), *Farmers first* (New York: Bootstrap Press, 1989).

Chambers, R. and M. Leach, 'Trees as savings and security for the rural poor', *World Development* **17**: 329–342 (1989).

Chapman, G. W. and T. G. Allan, *Establishment techniques for forest plantations* (Rome: FAO Forestry Paper 8, 1978).

Cheliak, W. M. and D. L. Rogers, 'Integrating biotechnology into tree improvement programs', *Canadian J Forest Research* **20**: 452–463 (1990).

Chou, C. K. S., 'Monoculture, species diversification, and disease hazards in forestry', *New Zealand J Forestry* **26**: 20–36 (1981).

Clarke, I. F., *The Pattern of Expectations: 1644-2001* (London: Jonathan Cape, 1979).

Clay, J. W., *Indigenous Peoples and Tropical Forests*, Cambridge, MA: Cultural Survival (1988).

Clutter, J. L., J. C. Fortson, L. V. Pienar, G. H. Brister and R. L. Bailey, *Timber management: a quantitative approach* (New York: Wiley, 1983).

Cocklin, C. R., 'Methodological problems in evaluating sustainability', *Environmental Conservation* **16**: 343–351 (1989).

CODEFF (Comite Nacional pro Defensa de la Fauna y Flora) Position paper on the Forest Policy Draft released by the World Bank on April 1, 1991 (unpublished, 1991).

Cook, C. C. and M. Grut, *Agroforestry in sub-Saharan Africa* (Washington, DC: World Bank, Technical Paper No. 112, 1989).

Cotterill, P. P., 'Genetic gains expected from alternative breeding strategies including simple low cost options', *Silvae Genetica* **35**: 212–223 (1986).

Cotterill, P. P., Personal communication (Obidos, Portugal: CELBI, 1992).

Countryside and Forestry Commissions (UK), *Forests for the community* (London: Countryside Commission, 1991).

Craib, I. J., *Thinning, pruning and management studies on the main exotic confiers grown in South Africa* (Pretoria, South Africa: Government Printer, Department of Agriculture and Forestry Science Bulletin 196, 1939).

Craib, I. J., *Silviculture of Exotic Conifers in South Africa*, British Empire Forestry Conference Papers (1947).

Dargavel, J. and S. Kengen, 'Promise and Performance of Industrial Plantations in Two Regions of Australia and Brazil', in: Steen, H. K. and Tucker, R. P. (eds) *Changing Tropical Forests: Historical Perspectives on Today's Challenges in Central and South America*, Forest History Society (1992).

Dargavel, J. (ed.), *Prospects for Australian plantation forests* (Canberra: Centre for Resource and Environmental Studies, Australian National University, 1990).

Davidson, J., *Bioenergy tree plantations in the tropics: ecological impacts and their implications* (Gland, Switzerland: IUCN Commission on Ecology, Paper No. 12, 1987).

Davis-Case, D., *Community forestry: participatory assessment, monitoring and evaluation* (Rome: FAO, Community Forestry Note 2, 1989).

Dawkins, H. C., 'Productivity of tropical rain forests and their ulitmate value to man', in: *The ecology of man in the tropical environment* (Morges, Switzerland: IUCN Publications New Series 4, 1967).

Dawkins, H. C., 'The first century of tropical silviculture: successes forgotten and failures misunderstood', in: *Oxford Rainforest Conference Proceedings* (Oxford: Oxford Forestry Institute, 1988).

Dawkins, H. C., Personal communication (Oxford: Oxford Forestry Institute, 1992).

Dean, W., 'The Tasks of Latin American Environmental History', in: Steen, H. K. and R. P. Tucker (eds) *Changing Tropical Forests: Historical Perspectives on Today's Challenges in Central and South America*, Forest History Society (1992).

Delwaulle, J. C., 'Plantations clonales d'*Eucalyptus* hybrides au Congo', *Bois et Forêts des Tropiques* **208**: 37–42 (1985).

Denslow, J. S. and C. Padoch, *People of the Tropical Rain Forest*, (Berkeley: University of California Press, 1988).

Deweess, P. A., *The impact of capital and labour availability on smallholder tree growing in Kenya* (Oxford: Department of Plant Sciences, Oxford University, unpublished D.Phil. thesis, 1991).

Dickson, D. A. and P. S. Savill, 'Early growth of *Picea sitchensis* on deep oligotrophic peat in Northern Ireland', *Forestry* **47**: 57–88 (1974).

Douglas, J. J., *A re-appraisal of forestry development in developing countries* (The Hague, Netherlands: Martinus Nijhoff/Dr W. Junk Publishers, 1983).

Douglas, J. J., 'Forestry and rural people: new economic perspectives', in: *Proceedings, Division 4, 18th IUFRO World Congress* (Ljubljana, Yugoslavia, September 1986), pp. 62–71.

Duryea, M. L. and P. M. Dougherty (eds), *Forest regeneration manual* (Dordrecht, Netherlands: Kluwer Academic Publishers, 1990).

Dykstra, D. P., *Mathematical programming for natural resource management* (New York: McGraw-Hill, 1984).

ECE/FAO, *European Timber Trends and Prospects to the Year 2000 and Beyond* (2 vols, New York: United Nations, 1986).

Elliott, D. A., R. N. James, D. W. McLean and W. R. J. Sutton, 'Financial returns from plantation forestry in New Zealand', in: *Proceedings of the 13th Commonwealth Forestry Conference*, **6C**, (Rotorua, New Zealand, September 1989).

Evans, J., *Plantation Silviculture in the Tropics*, (Oxford: Clarendon Press, 1982).

Evans, J., *Tropical Tree Plantations: Issues in 1990*. Consultancy report to IIED (1990).

Evans, J., *Plantation forestry in the tropics* (Oxford: Clarendon Press, 2nd edn, 1992).

Evans, J. and Wright, D., 'Usutu Forest Pulp Mill, Swaziland', in: *The Greening of Aid*, Conroy, C. and M. Litvinoff (eds) (London: Earthscan, 1988).

Evelyn, J., *Sylva or a Discourse of Forest Trees, and the Propagation of Timber in His Majesties Dominions* (1664) (o.p.).

FAO, *Poplars and Willows in Wood Production and Land Use* (Rome: FAO, 1980).

FAO, *Tree growing by rural people* (Rome: FAO, Forestry Paper 64, 1985a).

FAO, *A guide to forest seed handling* (Rome: FAO, Forestry Paper 20/2, 1985b).

FAO, *Forest Products: World Outlook Projections* (Rome: FAO, Forestry Paper 73, 1986).

FAO, *Appropriate wood harvesting in plantation forests* (Rome: FAO, Forestry Paper 78, 1987).

FAO, *Forest Products: World Outlook Projections* (Rome: FAO, Forestry Paper 84, 1988).

FAO, *Management of Tropical Moist Forests in Africa* (Rome: FAO, 1989).

FAO, *Household food security and forestry* (Rome: FAO, 1989a).

Farrell, P. W., 'Radiata pine residue management and its implications for site productivity on sandy soils', *Australian Forestry* 47: 95–102 (1984).

Felker, P., 'Uses of tree legumes in semi-arid areas', *Economic Botany* 35: 174–186 (1981).

FERIC, *Annual report 1991* (Point Clair, Quebec: Forest Engineering Research Institute of Canada, 1991).

Foley, G. and G. Barnard, *Farm and community forestry*, Network Paper no. 1b, Social Forestry Network, Overseas Development Institute, UK (1985).

Ford-Robinson, F.C. (ed.), *Terminology of forest science, technology, practice and products* (Washington, DC: Society of American Foresters, Multilingual Forestry Terminology Series 1, 1971).

Forest Ecology and Management 35(1,2) Special issue – conservation of diversity in forest ecosystems (1990).

Forestry Commission of Tasmania, *Forest practices code* (Hobart, Tasmania: Forestry Commission of Tasmania, 1989).

Formby, J., *Approaches to social impact assessment* (Canberra: Centre for Resource and Environmental Studies, Australian National University, Working Paper 1986/8, 1986).

Foster, P. G. and A. Constantini, 'Pinus plantation establishment in Queensland: I – Field surveys for site preparation planning and site design; II – Site preparation classes; III – Site preparation design, *Australian Forestry*, vol. 54 (1991), pp.75–94.

Franklin, E. C., 1989, 'Selection strategies for eucalypt tree improvement – four generations of selection in *Eucalyptus grandis* demonstrates valuable methodology', in: Gibson, G. L., A. R. Griffin and A. C. Matheson (eds), *Breeding tropical trees* (Oxford and Arlington, VA: Oxford Forestry Institute and Winrock International, 1989), pp. 197–209.,

Fuller, M., *Forest fires: an introduction to wildland fire behaviour, management, firefighting, and prevention* (New York: Wiley, 1991).

Galbraith, J. K., *The Affluent Society* (Boston: Houghton Mifflin, 1958).

Gauthier, J. J., 'Les bois de plantation dans le commerce mondial des produits forestiers', in: *L'émergence des nouveaux potentiels forestiers dans le monde* (Paris, France: AFOCEL, 1991), pp. 9–20.

Gibson, G. L., A. R. Griffin and A. C. Matheson (eds), *Breeding tropical trees* (Oxford and Arlington, VA: Oxford Forestry Institute and Winrock International, 1989b), pp. 148–158.

Gibson, G. L., R. D. Barnes and J. S. Berrington, 'Provenance productivity in *Pinus caribaea* and its interaction with environment', *Commonwealth Forestry Review* **62**: 93–106 (1983).

Gilmour, D. A., G. C. King and M. Hobley, 'Management of forests for local use in the hills of Nepal. 1. Changing forest management paradigms', *J World Forest Resource Management* **4**: 93–110 (1989).

Gilmour, D.A., G. C. King, G. B. Applegate and B. Mohns, 'Silviculture of plantation forests in central Nepal to maximise community benefits', *Forest Ecology and Management* **32**: 173–186 (1990).

Gondard, P., 'Land use in the Andean region of Ecuador', *Land Use Policy* **65**: 341–348 (1988).

Goodland, R., E. Asibey, J. Post and M. Dyson, *Tropical Moist Forest Hardwoods: the Urgent Transition to Sustainability*: paper presented to the International Society for Ecological Economics conference, 21–23 May 1990, 'The Ecological Economics of Sustainability', World Bank, Washington DC (1990).

Government of Japan, *Basic Plan for Japan's Forest Resources* and *Long Range Demand and Supply Projections for Important Forest Products* (Tokyo: Ministry of Agriculture, Forestry and Fisheries, 1980).

Grainger, A., 'Constraints on increasing tropical forest area to combat global climatic change', in: *Proceedings: Technical Workshop to explore options for global forestry management* (Bangkok, Thailand: IIED, ITTO and ONEB, 1991), pp. 196–208.

Greaves, A. and P. S. McCarter, *Cordia alliodora: a promising tree for tropical agroforestry* (Oxford: Oxford Forestry Institute, Tropical Forestry Papers No. 22, 1990).

Greenwood, E. A. N., L. Klein and J. D., Beresford, 'Differences in annual evaporation between grazed pasture and *Eucalpytus* species in plantations on a saline farm catchment', *J. Hydrology Neths* 78: 261–278 (1985).

Gregerson, H., S. Draper and D. Elz, *People and Trees: the role of social forestry in sustainable development*, Economic Development Institute of the World Bank, Washsington DC (1989).

Griffin, D. M., *Innocents abroad in the forests of Nepal: an account of Australian aid to Nepalese forestry* (Canberra: Australian National University, 1988).

Griffith, A. L., *Teak Plantation Techniques*, Indian Forest Record 5 (1942).

Grove, R., 'The origins of environmentalism', *Nature* v.345 3 (May 1990).

Hamilton, L. S. and Pearce, A. J., 'What are the soil and water benefits of planting trees in developing country watersheds?', in: *Sustainable resource development in the Third World*, D. D. Southgate and John Disinger (eds) (1987).

Harper, J. L., *Population Biology of Plants* (London: Academic Press, 1977).

Harwood, C. E., *Grevillea robusta: an annotated bibliography* (Nairobi, Kenya: ICRAF, 1989).

Haugen, D.A., 'Control procedures for *Sirex noctilio* in the Green Triangle: review from detection to severe outbreak', *Australian Forestry* 53: 24–32 (1990).

Heartwell, C., *A forest tenure system for the Yukon* (Victoria, British Columbia: Forestry Canada, 1988).

Hibberd, B. G. (ed.), *Forestry practice* (London: HMSO, UK Forestry Commission Handbook 6, 1991).

Hoekstra, D. A., 'Economics of agroforestry', *Agroforestry Systems* 5: 293–300 (1987).

Hoskings, G. P. and P. D. Gadgil, 'Forest insect and disease protection in New Zealand: an integrated approach', *Australian Forestry* 50: 37–39 (1987).

Hoskins, W. G., *The Making of the English Landscape* (London: Hodder and Stoughton, 1955).

Hughes, C. E., 'New opportunities in *Leucaena* genetic improvement', in: Gibson, G. L., A. R. Griffin and A. C. Matheson (eds), *Breeding tropical trees* (Oxford and Arlington, VA: Oxford Forestry Institute and Winrock International, 1989), pp. 218–226.

Hummel, F. C., 'Comparisons of forestry in Britain and mainland Europe', *Forestry* 64: 141–155 (1991).

Hurditch, W. J., *Problems of public forestry and the socio-economic impacts of privatisation* (Oxford: Oxford Forestry Institute Occasional Paper, 1992).

Huxley, A., *Plant and Planet* (London: Penguin, 1978).

Hyams, H. E., *Soil and Civilization* (London and New York: Thames and Hudson, 1952).

Hyde, W. F. and J. E. Seve, *Malawi: A rapid economic appraisal of smallholders' response to severe deforestation*: Proceedings of the 10th World Forestry Congress, Paris, September 1991, University of Washington.

Hyman, E.L. and B. Stiftel, *Combining facts and values in environmental impact assessment* (Boulder, CO: Westview Press, Social Impact Assessment Series No. 16, 1988).

ILO, *Tree nurseries: an illustrated guide and training manual* (Geneva, Switzerland: International Labour Organization and UNDP, Booklet No. 6, 1990).

Indian Forester, Forest corporations special issue, 117(9) (1991).

ITTO, *ITTO guidelines for the sustainable management of natural tropical forests* (Yokohama: International Tropical Timber Council, Technical Series 5, 1990).

ITTO, *Draft report of Working Group on ITTO guidelines for the establishment and sustainable management of planted tropical forests* (Yokohama: International Tropical Timber Council, 1991).

IUCN/UNEP/WWF, *Caring for the Earth. A strategy for sustainable living*, Munro D. and Holdgate M. W. (eds) (London: Earthscan, 1991).

James, N. D. G., *A History of English Forestry* (Oxford: Basil Blackwell, 1981).

Jellicoe, G. and S. Jellicoe, *The Landscape of Man* (London: Thames and Hudson, 1975).

Jodha, N. S., 'Sustainable land use involving trees in Himalayan Region: Perspectives and Policy Implications', in: *Report of an International Workshop on Forestry and Agroforestry Policy Research* (Washington: IFPRI, 1991).

Johnson, B., *Tree plantations, forest plantations and natural forest: a distinction between different concepts*: paper for Centre for Applied Studies in International Negotiations, 'Symposium on Tree Plantations: Benefits and Drawbacks', Geneva (April 1991).

Johnson, D. R., A. J. Grayson and R. T. Bradley, *Forest planning* (London: Faber and Faber, 1967).

Kallio, M., D. P. Dykstra and C. S. Blinkley, 'Introduction', in: Kallio, M., D. P. Dykstra and C. S. Blinkley (eds), *The global forest sector: an analytical perspective* (New York: Wiley-Interscience, 1987).

Kang, H. and H. Nienstaedt, 'Managing long-term breeding stock', *Silvae Genetica* 36: 30–39 (1987).

Kanowski, P. J. and D. G. Nikles, 'A summary of plans for continuing genetic improvement of *Pinus caribaea* var. *hondurensis* in Queensland', in: Gibson, G. L., A. R. Griffin and A. C. Matheson (eds), *Breeding tropical trees* (Oxford and Arlington, VA: Oxford Forestry Institute and Winrock International, 1989), pp. 236–249.

Kanowski, P. J. and P. S. Savill, *Plantation Forestry*, World Bank Forestry Policy Issues Paper (Oxford: Oxford Forestry Institute, 1990).

Kanowski, P. J., R. R. Woolaston and D. G. Nikles, 'Preliminary results of the OFI second stage provenance trial of *Pinus caribaea* var. *hondurensis* in Queensland', in: Gibson, G.L., A. R. Griffin and A. C. Matheson (eds), *Breeding tropical trees* (Oxford and Arlington, VA: Oxford Forestry Institute and Winrock International, 1989), pp. 377–378.

Keresztesi, B., 'Breeding and cultivation of black locust in Hungary', *Forest Ecology and Management* 30: 217–244 (1983).

King, K. F. S., 'The History of Agroforestry', in Nair, P. K. R., *Agroforestry Systems in the Tropics* (Dordrecht: Kluwer Academic Publishers, 1989).

Kirkland, A., 'The rise and fall of multiple use management in New Zealand', *New Zealand Forestry* 33(1): 9–12 (1989).

Kitzmiller, J. H., 'Managing genetic diversity in a tree improvement program', *Forest Ecology and Management* 35: 131–150 (1990).

Knopp, T. B. and E. S. Caldbeck, 'The role of participatory democracy in forest management', *J Forestry* 88(5): 13–18 (1990).

Kondas, S., '*Casuarina equisetifolia* – a multipurpose cash crop in India', in: Midgley, S. J., J. W. Turnbull and R. D. Johnston (eds), *Casuarina ecology, management, and utilisation* (Canberra, Australia: CSIRO Division of Forest Research, 1981).

Kotari, K., *Initial Hardships of the Japanese State Forest in late nineteenth century*: voluntary paper for ITTO Conference of Senior Foresters, Yokohama (1991).

Lagercrantz, K., 'The Wuvalu Cooperative Plantation: a case study', in Walter (ed.) (1981).

Lamb, D., *Exploiting the tropical rain forest: an account of pulpwood logging in Papua New Guinea*, Man and the Biosphere Series no. 3, Unesco (1990).

Lamprecht, H., *Silviculture in the tropics* (Hamburg: Verlag Paul Harey, 1986; English edn 1990).

Langlands, B. W., 'Burning in Eastern Africa with particular reference to Uganda', *East African Geographical Review* 5: 22 (1967).

Langley, B., *Sure Method of Improving Estates by plantation of oak, elm, ash, beech and other timber trees, copppice woods . . .* (1728).

Latham, R. (translator), *Marco Polo: the Travels* (Harmondsworth: Penguin, 1958).

Leach, G. and R. Mearns, *Beyond the woodfuel crisis* (London: Earthscan, 1988).

Lear, D. H. van and T. A. Waldrop, 'Prescribed burning for regeneration', in: Duryea, M. L. and P. M. Dougherty (eds), *Forest regeneration manual* (Dordrecht, Netherlands: Kluwer Academic Publishers, 1990).

Leslie, A. J., 'Economic feasibility of natural management of tropical forests', in: Mergen, F. R. and J. R. Vincent (eds), *Natural management of tropical moist forests* (New Haven, CT: School of Forestry and Environmental Studies, Yale University, 1987), pp. 177–198.

Leslie, A. J., *Measures to Strengthen Environmentally Sound Sustainable Management of Timber Resources for Secondary Wood Processing Industry* (Vienna: 2nd World Consultation on Wood Industry, UNIDO, 1991).

Leuschner, W. A., *Introduction to forest resource management* (New York: Wiley, 1984).

Liew That Chim (ed.), *Proceedings: seminar on forest plantation development in Malaysia* (Kota Kinabalu, Sabah: Forest Department, Sabah, 1984).

Lohmann, L., 'Commercial tree plantations in Thailand: deforestation by any other name', *The Ecologist* vol. 20 no. 1 (1990).

Lundgren, B. O. and J. B. Raintree, 'Sustained Agroforestry' in: Nestel, B. (ed.), *Agricultural research for development: potentials and challenges in Asia*, ISNAR (1982).

MacGillivray, A. W., *Forest Use and Conflict in Burma 1750–1990*, thesis, Imperial College, University of London (1990).

Malcolm, D. C., 'The future development of even-aged plantations: silvicultural implications', in: Ford, E. D., D. C. Malcolm and J. Atterson (eds), *Ecology of even-aged forest plantations* (Cambridge: Institute of Terrestrial Ecology, 1979), pp. 481–504.

Manion, P. D., *Tree disease concepts* (Englewood Cliffs, NJ: Prentice-Hall, 2nd edn, 1991).

Marchak, M. P., 'Latin America and the Creation of a Global Forest Industry', in: Steen, H. K. and R. P. Tucker (eds), *Changing Tropical Forests: Historical Perspectives on Today's Challenges in Central and South America*, Forest History Society (1992).

Maser, C., *The redesigned forest* (Toronto: Stoddart, 1990).

Mather, A. S., *Global Forest Resources* (London: Belhaven Press, 1990).

McCracken, J. A., J. N. Pretty and G. R. Conway, *An introduction to rapid rural appraisal* (London: IIED, 1988).

McGaughey, S. E. and H. M. Gregersen, *Investment policies and financing mechanisms for sustainable forestry development* (Washington, DC: Inter-American Development Bank, 1988).

Malaysian Timber Industry Board, *Malaysian rubberwood* (Kuala Lumpur: MTIB, 1988).

Mengin-Lecreux, P. and P. Durand, 'Economic approaches to the development of the forest plantation sector, with special reference to the experience of France and French-speaking Africa', in: *Proceedings of Conference on the future role of forest plantations in the national economy and incentives required to encourage investments in forest plantation development*, Tang, Pinso Marsh and Sabah (eds) in collaboration with Tropenbos (1987).

Midgley, S. J., *The Australian Tree Seed Centre: a window to the resource* (Canberra, Australia: CSIRO Division of Forestry, 1988).

Miller, H. G., 'Forestry fertilization: some guiding concepts', *Forestry* 54: 157–167 (1981).

Molnar, A., *Community forestry - a review* (Rome: FAO, Community Forestry Note 3, 1989).

Moran, G. F. and J. C. Bell, 'The origin and genetic diversity of *Pinus radiata* in Australia', *Theoretical and Applied Genetics* 73: 616–622 (1987).

Namkoong, G., 'Systems of gene management', in: Gibson, G. L., A. R. Griffin and A. C. Matheson (eds), *Breeding tropical trees* (Oxford and Arlington, VA: Oxford Forestry Institute and Winrock International, 1989), pp. 1–8.

Namkoong, G., H. C. Kang and J. S. Brouard, *Tree breeding: principles and strategies* (New York: Springer-Verlag, 1988).

Namkoong, G., R. D. Barnes and J. Burley, *A philosophy of breeding strategy for tropical forest trees* (Oxford: Commonwealth Forestry Institute, Tropical Forestry Papers No. 16, 1980).

National Research Council (USA), *Managing global genetic resources - tropical forest trees*, Commonwealth Forestry Institute, University of Oxford (Washington, DC: Tropical Forestry Papers No. 16., p. 67 National Academy Press, 1991).

New Larousse, *Encyclopaedia of Mythology* (1968).

New Zealand Government Ministry of External Relations and Trade, Development Assistance Division, *The appropriateness of industrial plantation development in delivering New Zealand official development assistance* (1989).

Osako, M. M., 'Forest preservation in Tokugawa Japan', in: Tucker, R. P. and Richards, J. F. (eds), *Global Deforestation and the Nineteenth Century World Economy* (Durham: Duke Press Policy Series, 1983).

Palmer, J. R., 'Case study – JARI: lessons for land managers in the tropics'. Paper for *International workshop on rainforest regeneration and management* (Guri, Venezuela: 1986).

Palmer, J. R., 'Management of natural forest for sustainable timber production: a commentary', Chapter 6 in: Poore, D. (ed.), *No timber without trees - sustainability in the tropical forest* (London: Earthscan, 1989), pp. 154–189.

Palmer, J. R. and T. J. Synnott, *The management of national forests*. Issues Paper for the World Bank Forestry Policy Review (1991).

Pereira, H. and J. Santos Pereira, 'Short rotation biomass plantations in Portugal' in: Hummel, F. C., W. Palz and G. Grassi (eds), *Biomass forestry in Europe: a strategy for the future* (London: Elsevier Applied Science, 1988), pp. 509–539.

Perlin, J., *A Forest Journey: The Role of Wood in the Development of Civilization* (New York: W. W. Norton, 1989).

Poffenberger, M., *Joint Management for Forest Lands: Experiences from South Asia* (New Delhi: Ford Foundation, 1990).

Poore, M. E. D. and C. Fries, *The ecological effects of Eucalyptus*: FAO Forestry Paper 59 (Rome: FAO, 1985).

Poore, M. E. D. (ed.), *No timber without trees - sustainability in the tropical forest* (London: Earthscan, 1989).

Poore, M. E. D. and J. Sayer, *The management of tropical moist forest lands: ecological guidelines* (Gland, Switzerland: IUCN, 1987).

Price, C., *Time, discounting and value* (Oxford: Basil Blackwell, in press).

Pryor, S. N. and P. S. Savill, *Silvicultural systems for broadleaved woodlands in Britain* (Oxford: Oxford Forestry Institute, Occasional Papers No. 32, 1986).

Purse, J. G., 'Development of techniques for vegetative propagation in Pines - a review of progress and prospects', in: Gibson, G. L., A. R. Griffin and A. C. Matheson (eds), *Breeding tropical trees* (Oxford and Arlington, VA: Oxford Forestry Institute and Winrock International, 1989), pp. 298-310.

Pyne, S. J., *Introduction to wildland fire: fire management in the United States* (New York: Wiley, 1984).

Queensland Department of Forestry, *Aspects of management of plantations in tropical and sub-tropical Queensland* (Brisbane, Australia: Department of Forestry, Queensland, 1987).

Queensland Department of Forestry, *Plantation establishment* [mimeo] (Brisbane, Australia: Queensland Department of Forestry, 1989).

Raintree, J. B., 'The state of the art of agroforestry diagnosis and design', *Agroforestry Systems* 5: 219-250 (1987).

Randall, A., *Resource economics* (New York: Wiley, 2nd edn, 1987).

Remrod, J., *Clearcutting and silviculture: the Swedish example*: paper for the 71st Annual metting of the Woodlands Section, CPAA (Montreal: Canadian Forest Industries, 1989).

Rickman, R., *What's good for woods* (London: Centre for Policy Studies, Policy Study No. 129, 1991).

Rietbergen, S., 'Africa' in Poore, D. (ed.), *No Timber Without Trees: Sustainability in the Tropical Forest* (London: Earthscan, 1989).

Risby, A. E., 'Realities of timber production', Chapter 16 in: Dargavel, J. and G. Sheldon (eds), *Prospects for Australian hardwood forests* (Canberra: Centre for Resource and Environmental Studies, Australian National University, Monograph 19, 1987), pp. 213-220.

Rogaly, B., *Lathur rural development project evaluation report*: report to Friends of ASSEFA (London, 1991).

Romm, J., 'Forestry for development: some lessons from Asia', *J World Forest Resource Management* 4: 37-46 (1989).

Romm, J., 'Exploring institutional options for global forest management', in: *Proceedings: Technical Workshop to explore options for global forestry management* (Bangkok, Thailand: IIED, ITTO and ONEB, 1991), pp. 186-192.

Rosenberg, N. J., *Microclimate: the biological environment* (New York: Wiley, 1974).

Sargent, C., *Land Use Issues*, Report for Papua New Guinea Tropical Forest Action Programme (1989).

Sargent, C., *The Khun Song Plantation Project: a socioeconomic and environmental analysis and recommendations towards the establishment and management of a plantation in Chantaburi Province by Shell Companies of Thailand* (London: IIED, 1990).

Sargent, C., *Defining the Issues* (London: IIED, 1990b).

Sargent, C., *Vietnam Forestry Sector Review: Land Use Issues*. MOF/UNDP/FAO. VIE/88/037 (London: IIED, 1991).

Sargent, C. and S. Bass, 'The Future Shape of Forests', in: Holmberg, J. (ed.), *Policies for a Small Planet* (London: Earthscan, 1992).

Savill, P. S. and P. J. Kanowski, *Tree improvement programmes of European species: goals and strategies* (Nogent sur Vernisson, France: paper presented at Meeting on Genetics and Breeding of Oaks, September, 1991).

Savill, P. S. and J. Evans, *Plantation silviculture in temperate regions* (Oxford: Clarendon Press, 1986).

Saxena, N. C., 'Marketing constraints for *Eucalyptus* from farm lands in India', *Agroforestry Systems* 13: 73–86 (1991).

Sayer, J., *Rainforest buffer zones: Guidelines for protected area managers* (Gland: IUCN, 1991).

Sayer, J. A. and T. C. Whitmore, 'Tropical moist forests: destruction and species extinction', *Biological Conservation* 55: 199–213 (1991).

Schmidheiny, S. and Business Council for Sustainable Development, *Changing Course: A Global Business Perspective on Development and the Environment* (Cambridge: MIT Press, 1992).

Sedjo, R. A., 'Forest resources of the world: forests in transition', Chapter 1 in: Kallio, M., D. P. Dykstra and C. S. Blinkley (eds), *The global forest sector: an analytical perspective* (New York: Wiley-Interscience, 1987), pp. 7–31.

Shell, *Environmental auditing guide* (The Hague, Netherlands: Shell Petroleum, 1989).

Shiva, V., *Forestry crisis and forestry myths* (Penang, Malaysia: World Rainforest Movement, 1987).

Shiva, V. and J. Bandyopadhyay, 'Asia's Forest Cultures', in: Head, S. and R. Heinzman, *Lessons of the Rainforest* (San Francisco: Sierra Club Books, 1990).

Shiva, V., J. Bandyopadhyay and N. D. Jayal, 'Afforestation in India: problems and strategies', *Ambio* 14 no. 6 (1985).

Simpson, J. A. and M. J. Grant, *Exotic pine fertilizer practice and its development in Queensland* (Brisbane, Australia: Queensland Forest Service, Technical Paper No. 49, 1991).

Simpson, J. A. and P. K. Ades, 'Screening *Pinus radiata* families and clones for disease and pest insect resistance', *Australian Forestry* 53: 194–199.

Spears, J., *Plantation Forestry in Developing Countries: Equity, Environmental and Economic Concerns*: discussion Paper for CASIN Symposium on Tree Plantations, Geneva (1991).

Speight, M. R. and D. Wainhouse, *Ecology and management of forest insects* (Oxford: Clarendon Press, 1989).

Spilsbury, M. J., *Modelling the development of mixed deciduous woodland ecosystems* (Oxford: Department of Plant Sciences, Oxford University, unpublished D.Phil. thesis, 1990).

Srivastavea, H. C., B. Vatsya and K. K. G. Menon (eds), *Plantation crops: opportunities and constraints* (New Delhi, India: Oxford and IBH Publishing, 1986).

Staaf, K. A. G. and N. A. Wiksten, *Tree harvesting techniques* (Dordrecht, Netherlands: Martinus Nijhoff/Dr W. Junk Publishers, 1984).

Stewart, P. J., *Growing against the grain* (Oxford: Council for the Protection of Rural England, 1987).

Streets, R. J., *Exotic forest trees in the British Commonwealth* (Oxford: Clarendon Press, 1962).

Sturm, J., 'Panorama des nouveaux potentials forestiers de l'hémisphère sud: origine, problématique, impact', in: *L'émergence des nouveaux potentiels forestiers dans le monde* (Paris, France: AFOCEL, 1991), pp. 35-50.

Sutton, W. R. J., 'Are we too concerned about wood production?', *New Zealand Forestry* 36(3): 25-28 (1991).

Tannahill, R., *Food in History* (London: Penguin, 1988).

Thirgood, J. V., *Man and the Mediterranean Forest: a History of Resource Depletion* (London and New York: Academic Press, 1981).

Tho, Y. P., 'Tropical moist forests – facts and issues', in: *Proceedings of the technical workshop to explore options for global forest management* (Bangkok, Thailand: IIED, ITTO and ONEB, 1991).

Thomas, K., *Man and the Natural World: Changing Attitudes in England 1500-1800* (London: Allen Lane, 1983).

Thompson, M., M. Warburton and T. Hatley, *Uncertainty on a Himalayan scale* (London: Milton Ash, 1986).

Thompson, M. A., 'Determining impact significance in EIA: a review of 24 methodologies', *J Environmental Management* 30: 235-250 (1990).

Tiffen, M. and M. Mortimore, *Theory and Practice in Plantation Agriculture: an economic review* (London: Overseas Development Institute, 1990).

Tomkins, J., 'Recreation and the Forestry Commission: the case for multiple-use resource management within public forestry in the UK', *J Environmental Management* 30: 79-88 (1990).

Tompkins, S., *Forestry in Crisis* (London: Christopher Helm, 1989).

Tucker, R. P. and J. F. Richards (eds), *Global Deforestation and the Nineteenth Century World Economy* (Durham: Duke Press Policy Series, 1983).

van Ginneken, P., *Not seeing the people for the trees: A review of practices and policies of tree planting* (Amsterdam: AIDEnvironment, 1992).

Vaux, H. J. and J. A. Zivnuska, 'Forest Production Goals: A Critical Analysis', *Land Economics* 28(4): 318–327 (1952).

Veblen, T., *The Theory of the Leisure Class* (London, Allen & Unwin, 1957).

Weiskel, T. C., 'The Anthropology of Environmental Decline: Historical Aspects of Anthropogenic Ecological Degradation', *Reference Services Review*, USA (Summer 1990).

Weiskel, T. C., 'Rubbish and Racism: Problems of Boundary in an Ecosystem', *Yale Review* 72:2 (1983).

Westoby, J. C., Forest Industries in the Attack on Underdevelopment, *Unasylva* 16(4), (1962).

Westoby, J. C., 'Forest Industries for Socio-economic Development', *Y Coedwigwr* no. 31 (1975).

Westoby, J. C., *Forest Industries for Socio-Economic Development* Proc. Eighth World Forestry Congress, Jakarta (1978).

Westoby, J. C., *The purpose of forests* (Oxford: Basil Blackwell, 1987).

Westoby, J. C., 'The role of forest industries in the attack on economic underdevelopment' (1962), in: Westoby, J. C., *The purpose of forests* (Oxford: Basil Blackwell, 1987), pp. 3–70.

Westoby, J. C., 'Responsibility' (1974), reprinted as Chapter 10 in: *The Purpose of Forests* (Oxford: Blackwell, 1987).

White, T. L., 'A conceptual framework for tree improvement programs', *New Forests* 1: 325–342 (1987).

Whitehead, D., 'An ecological overview of plantation forestry', *New Zealand J Forestry* 26: 14–19 (1981).

Whitehead, D., 'Ecological aspects of natural and plantation forests', *Forestry Abstracts* 43: 615–624 (1982).

Whiteside, I. D., 'Economic advances made in New Zealand Radiata Pine plantation forestry since the early 1980s', in: *Proceedings of the 13th Commonwealth Forestry Conference*, 6C (Rotorua, New Zealand, September 1989).

Whyte, A. G. D., 'Radiata pine silviculture in New Zealand: its evolution and future prospects', *Australian Forestry* 51: 185–196 (1988).

Whyte, A. G. D., 'Planning and control of forest operations in New Zealand plantations', in: Pritchard, M. A. (ed.), *A systems approach to forest operations planning and control* (London: HMSO, UK Forestry Commission Bulletin 82, 1989), pp. 10–18.

Wilkinson, G. R. and W. A. Neilsen, 'Effects of herbicides on woody weed control and growth of plantation eucalypt seedlings', *Australian Forestry* 53: 69–78 (1990).

Wilkinson, G., *Epitaph for the Elm* (London: Hutchinson, 1978).

Williams, E., *From Columbus to Castro: the History of the Caribbean 1492–1969* (London: Andre Deutsch, 1970).

Wilson, R. A., Personal communication (Madrid, Spain: CEASA, 1992).

Wilson, R. V., 'Financial returns from plantation forestry in Australia', in: *Proceedings of the 13th Commonwealth Forestry Conference*, **6C** (Rotorua, New Zealand, September 1989).

Winpenny, J. T., *Values for the environment* (London: HMSO, 1991).

Wood, R. F. and M. Nimmo, *Chalk Downland Afforestation*, Forestry Commission Bulletin, No. 34 (London: HMSO, 1962).

World Bank, *The forest sector – a World Bank policy paper* (Washington, DC: World Bank, 1991).

Yoho, J. G., 'Continuing investments in forestry: private investment strategies', in: Sedjo, R. A. (ed.), *Investment in forestry* (Boulder, CO: Westview, 1985).

Young, C., Personal communication (Oxford: Landel Mills Commodity Studies, 1990).

Young, J., *Forestry lacks coherent policy* (London: *The Times*, 9th December 1991).

Zobel, B. J. and J. T. Talbert, *Applied forest tree improvement* (New York: Wiley, 1984).

Zobel, B. J., G. van Wyk and P. Stahl, *Growing exotic forests* (New York: Wiley-Interscience, 1987).

INDEX

acacias 29, 124, 130, 136
Acland Committee 54
Adlard, P. G. 42, 43, 47, 53, 59, 62, 132
agriculture 18, 20, 23, 36, 44, 46–8, 50, 87, 159, 161
agroforestry 39–40, 64–5, 102, 106, 117, 129, 161
Allan, T. G. 16, 140, 141
Aracruz Celulose S. A. 90–1
Arnold, J. E. M. 44, 65, 66, 85, 89, 95, 103, 105, 127, 129, 133, 148
Asibey, E. O. 86, 89
Australia 56–7, 125, 126, 144

Bangladesh 59, 126
Barnes, R. D. 138, 139, 144
Bass, S. M. J. 18, 116, 118
Bell, J. C. 134, 135
Binkley, C. S. 114, 124
biodiversity 12, 25–6, 26–7, 28, 30, 35, 36, 37, 138, 160, 164
biotechnology see genetics/ biotechnology
Boardman, R. 142, 143, 146
Brandis, D. 64
Brazil 41, 46, 62–3, 87, 90–1, 101, 102, 103, 125, 126, 146
Brunig, E. F. 27, 28
buffer zones 32
Burley, J. 91, 139
Burma 41, 49, 59, 63, 64, 73–5
Business Council for Sustainable Development 90, 91

Cameroon 26, 61
Camphinos, E. (Jr) 134, 146

carbon sequestration and storage 11, 21, 22, 36, 126, 162
Cartiere Burgo Society 71
Caufield, C. 94, 118
Central America 57, 123
Chambers, R. 98, 99, 101, 102, 107, 108, 110, 119, 127, 131
Chapman G. W. 140, 141
Cheliak, W. M. 137, 138
Chile 62, 87, 100, 101, 125, 126
China 16, 47, 103, 126
climate 21, 29–30, 140, 159
CODEFF 100, 101
Committee on Forest Development in the Tropics 153
complex plantations 24, 30, 39–40, 147–9, 150, 167, 168
conservation 12, 137
Consultative Group on International Agricultural Research (CGIAR) 135
corporations see private sector investment in plantations
Costa Rica 26, 135, 152–3
Cote d'Ivoire 35
Cotta 52
Cotterill, P. P. 125, 137
cultural and religious factors 43–4, 48–9, 67, 88, 93, 98, 112
cypresses 19

Dargavel, J. 45, 56, 57, 61, 62, 65, 149
Davis-Case, D. 130, 131
Dawkins, H. C. 19, 125
definitions 11, 17–19, 121–2
development assistance/aid 61, 65, 153–4
Dougherty, P. M. 137, 139, 140, 143

Douglas, J. J. 124, 148
Duryea, M. L. 137, 139, 140, 143

East Africa 19
economic development 20, 60–1, 65,
    124, 164
economics of plantations 19, 23, 35,
    38–9, 44–5, 61, 67, 73, 129, 158
Egypt 126
Elliott, D. A. 128, 129
employment 14, 56–7, 100–1, 114,
    126, 161, 164
energy 36, 45, 52–3, 62, 87, 125–6,
    161
England 49–56
environmental impacts of plantations
    12, 28, 34, 57, 131, 132, 154–5
environmental protection, plantations
    for 12, 21–2, 28, 56, 59, 67, 126,
    161, 162, 164
eucalyptus 20, 23, 28, 29, 59, 60, 62,
    63, 65, 90–1, 94, 117, 124, 128, 135,
    136, 149
Evans, J. 16, 26, 41, 100, 103, 121, 125,
    134, 137–42 passim, 144, 145, 148
Evelyn, John 50–1
exotic species, relation to indigenous
    species 93–4, 98, 137, 152

FAO 24, 65, 71, 77, 80, 99, 133, 139,
    146, 148, 153
Fiji 116, 126
financial factors 32, 44–5, 61, 67, 74,
    89, 126, 127, 128–9, 152, 158
fire 10, 141, 142, 144–5, 152, 154, 155
Food & Agriculture Organisation see
    FAO
forecasting wood demand 13–14, 19,
    24, 67–8, 76–8, 80–1 see also wood
    consumption and demand
Forestry Commission (Great Britain)
    54, 55, 149
Forestry Commission of Tasmania
    131, 132

Forestry Research Institute of Ghana
    152
France 56
fuelwood 30, 38–9, 53, 77, 82, 83, 84,
    87, 98, 99, 126, 153–4

Gabon 61
Gautier, J. J. 122, 123, 124, 147
gender issues 30, 66, 103, 118–20,
    155, 164
genetics/biotechnology 37, 134–8,
    151, 160, 164, 165
Germany 17
Ghana 30, 151–2
Gilmour, D. A. 129, 136, 148, 149
governments 88–9, 96, 104–5
Greece 47
Gregersen, H. M. 101, 127, 128, 129,
    131
Griffin, D. M. 31, 111, 148

Haiti 104, 108
Hibberd, B. G. 140, 144, 146
Home-Grown Timber (Acland)
    Committee 54
Hughes, C. E. 134, 136, 144
Huxley, A. 47, 48
Hyde, W. F. 38, 39

Ikemori, Y. K. 91, 134, 146
incentives 50–2, 58, 66, 67, 89, 94–6,
    109, 113, 115, 152, 157–8, 162 see
    also purposes of tree planting
India 16, 29, 43, 49, 58–9, 62, 66, 92,
    98, 99, 102, 103, 105, 106, 108, 126,
    127, 146
indigenous species 94, 137, 151–2
Indonesia 10, 58, 59, 105
industry 34, 52–3, 61, 67–8, 161, 164
information needs 112–13, 130–1,
    136, 152
infrastructure 10, 45, 101–2, 114, 159
Intergovernmental Panel on Climate
    Change (IPCC) 21

International Tropical Timber
Organisation (ITTO) 89, 131, 132,
151, 152
investment 17, 31, 33, 60, 127, 150,
163, 164 *see also* private sector
investment in plantations
Iran 47
Italy 49, 70–1

James, N. D. G. 50, 51, 53, 54, 55
Japan 17, 71–3, 80, 126
Java 10, 59, 105

Kanowski, P. J. 29, 35, 61, 62, 63, 65,
134, 137, 138
Kengen, S. 45, 56, 57, 61, 62, 65
Kenya 60, 103, 104, 126, 127
Korea 103

Lamprecht, H. 18
land use, competing demands in 30,
37, 42, 67, 97–8, 148, 157, 162, 163
landscape, aesthetics and recreation
30, 39, 43, 49, 54–6, 67, 98
Langley, Batty 51
Latin America 48, 57, 66, 86, 123
Leslie, A. J. 81, 128, 129
Leuschner, W. A. 133, 145
Liberia 61
Lohmann, L. 88, 90, 99, 104
Ludwig, Daniel 41, 62–3

McGaughey, S. E. 127, 128, 129, 131
mahogany 29
Malawi 38–9, 61, 101
Malaysia 124, 126
Malaysian Timber Industry Board 130
Mather, A. S. 88, 90, 122, 123
Menjin-Lecreux, P. 19, 35
monitoring 14, 115, 132–3, 166
Moran, G. F. 134, 135
Mortimore, M. 96, 105, 108
motivation *see* incentives; purposes of
tree planting
multi-purpose trees 161

multiple species 39, 168

Namkoong, G. 137, 138
National Research Council 134, 135
natural forests 12, 16, 17–18, 20, 23,
24, 25, 31–3, 37, 50, 58, 60, 125,
158–60, 167
Nepal 31, 102, 103, 126, 149
New Zealand 56, 62, 87, 116, 125,
126, 127, 128
non-governmental organisations
(NGOs) 107, 108, 109, 113
non-timber forest products 30–1
Noordwijk Convention 21, 23, 36, 162
North America 57, 62, 86, 123, 137
nutrients 142–3

Overseas Development
Administration 153, 154

Pakistan 59, 103
Palmer, J. R. 18, 26, 58
Paper Industry Corporation of the
Philippines 117–18
Papua New Guinea 10, 31, 99, 100
participation of people 88, 102–3,
108, 109–16, 117–18, 148, 164, 166
participatory/rapid rural appraisal
111, 116–17, 166
participatory (social) forestry 16, 65–
6, 68, 105–6, 155
Paulista Railway Company 62
Pereira, H. 125, 135, 146
Perlin, J. 41, 50, 52
pests, diseases and weeds 18–19, 63,
74, 131, 141–2, 144, 152, 154
Philippines 59, 104, 105, 117–18, 126
pine 10, 26–7, 56, 62, 63, 124, 128,
135, 149
planning of plantations 131
plantation area and resources 16–17,
20, 21–2, 122–3, 166
plantation types 11, 106–7
Poffenberger, M. 66, 113

policies 13, 20, 23, 32–3, 34, 149, 150, 158, 159, 160, 163, 169
Poore, M. E. D. 16, 29, 33, 132
poplars and willows 62, 69–71, 144
Portugal 94, 124, 146
private sector investment in plantations 20, 31, 33, 34, 40, 60, 61–2, 85–91, 105, 107, 108, 128–9, 158, 164, 168
production and productivity of plantations 12, 16, 122, 124, 125, 126, 127, 138, 159, 160
pulp and paper 11, 22, 28, 45, 61, 62–3, 77, 81–2, 83–4, 85, 87, 90–1, 117–18, 148–9
purposes of tree planting 22–3, 25, 46–9, 67, 124–7, 136, 157–8 see also incentives

Queensland Department of Forestry 131, 137, 139, 142, 144, 146

Raintree, J. B. 64, 132
research 54, 63, 65, 69, 101–11, 115, 150, 152, 165
Richards, J. F. 41, 73
Rietbergen, S. 35, 61
Rogers, D. L. 137, 138
Romm, J. 41, 146, 149

Santos Pereira, J. 125, 135, 146
Sargent, C. 18, 24, 28, 31, 35, 40, 94, 100, 129, 131, 148
Savill, P. S. 29, 35, 61, 62, 63, 65, 125, 137, 138, 139, 141, 143, 145
Sayer, J. A. 32, 132, 134
Schmidheiny, S. 61, 90, 91
Sedjo, R. A. 124
Seve, J. E. 38, 39
Shell Petroleum 40, 73, 87–8, 116, 118, 133
shifting agriculture/swidden 44, 46
silviculture of plantations 18, 19, 35, 129, 142, 143

simple plantations 24, 33, 147, 148, 149, 150, 167
site selection 33–4, 152
social factors 14, 15, 42–3, 88, 92–3, 109, 112, 155, 168–9
social forestry 16, 65–6, 68, 105–6, 155
social impacts of plantations 12, 30, 97–102, 108, 156–7, 164
social (participatory) forestry 16, 65–6, 68, 105–6, 155
social structures see social factors
soils 27–8, 74, 132, 140, 159
South Africa 56, 62
Spain 94, 149
Spears, J. 60, 106
Speight, M. R. 131, 144
staff, operational 165–6
sustainability 16, 24–5, 31, 35, 37, 88, 89, 90–1, 130, 146, 163–6
Sutton, W. R. J. 122, 123, 124
Swaziland 26, 62, 101, 103, 124
Sweden 23, 24
Switzerland 126
Syria 47

Tannahill, R. 46, 47
Tanzania 60, 104
taungya 10, 30, 64–5, 74, 106, 142, 148, 151, 161
teak 58–9, 60, 62, 64, 73–5
technology 45–6, 53, 63, 67, 86, 115, 130, 133–46, 164–5
tenure and rights 10, 14, 20, 23, 32, 34, 40, 42, 56, 66, 67, 68, 72, 96–7, 98, 100, 104, 105, 106, 112, 114, 115, 118, 149–50, 161, 163, 168
Thailand 20, 23, 74, 94, 105, 148–9
Thomas, K. 53, 54, 55
Tiffen, M. 96, 105, 108
trade 73, 74, 125, 158
Trinidad 59

Tropical Forest Action Programme 153, 154
Tucker, R. P. 41, 73

United Kingdom 124, 125, 126, 149
Usutu Pulp Company 62, 103

van Ginneken, P. 23, 107
Venezuela 125
Vietnam 10, 28, 29, 59, 99
Vincent, J. R. 114, 124

Wainhouse, D. 131, 144
war and military action 43, 51, 53–4, 58, 72, 73, 118
Waugh, G. 124, 146
weeds *see* pests, diseases and weeds

Westoby, J. C. 61, 65, 66, 79
Whiteside, I. D. 128, 138
Whitmore, T. C. 134
Whyte, A. G. D. 133, 143, 145
wood consumption and demand 10–11, 13–14, 44, 78–9, 83–4, 85, 167
see also forecasting wood demand
World Bank 65, 85–6, 90, 98, 106, 107, 122, 123
World Conservation Strategy 37
World Wide Fund for Nature 116

Zambia 60
Zimbabwe 125
Zobel, B. J. 134, 137, 138, 144